TITO

Other books by Milovan Djilas

The New Class
Conversations with Stalin
Montenegro
The Leper and Other Stories
Njegoš
The Unperfect Society
Under the Colors
Land Without Justice
The Stone and the Violets
Memoir of a Revolutionary
Parts of a Lifetime
Wartime

TITO

The Story from Inside

BY MILOVAN DJILAS

Translated by Vasilije Kojić and Richard Hayes

HBJ HARCOURT BRACE JOVANOVICH   NEW YORK AND LONDON

949.702
Dil

Library of Congress Cataloging in Publication Data

Dilas, Milovan.
Tito: the story from inside.
Translated from the Serbo-Croatian (Roman)
1. Tito, Josip Broz, Pres, Yugoslavia, 1892–1980   2.   Yugoslavia—
Presidents—Biography. 3. Dilas, Milovan.
4.   Statesmen—Yugoslavia—Biography.   5.   Yugoslavia—
Politics and government—1945–   I.   Title.
DR359.T5D5413   949.7′023′0924 [B]   80–23040
ISBN 0–15–190474–X

Printed in the United States of America

First edition

B C D E

TITO

1

How banal, yet irrefutable, is the assertion that man is a mixture of the "angelic" and the "demonic." When a man believes that either of these elements prevails, he is mistaken or he deceives himself. Most often the angelic and the demonic proceed together; between them there is a mutual interplay, in which the latter uses the former, while the former justifies the latter. Victory is sweetest for the man who acknowledges the duality of his nature. He can exercise this duality in the light of theoretical values he has inherited, or of those he has himself devised.

Nowhere is this demonstrated more powerfully, more completely, than in politics. Determining the life of a nation and a society—politics—is the fullest and highest form of human activity. In politics life is at its most concentrated. Lenin's view of politics was influenced by the dogma of the primacy of economics, but economic dogma did not deter him from becoming possibly one of the most totalitarian of politicians.

A true politician, a person of real flesh and blood, for whom politics is a vocation—whether it is a calling imposed on him by a higher life force or his unique creative gift—can be neither angelic nor demonic. His surmounting these simplistic definitions does not imply that the politician is a superman. He is not. He differs from others by possessing a more powerful political instinct, a gift with which others are also endowed, but to a lesser degree. No, a politician is neither "an angel" nor "a demon," neither instinctually good nor evil. He cannot be so if he is to exercise his political power responsibly, if he is to negotiate with courage and skill on the razor's edge between victory and defeat, life and death.

I do not consider these thoughts new. Anyone speaking after Aristotle and Machiavelli would be hard put to say anything new on the subject of politics. I do not intend to get involved with theory. Here I speak from personal experience and knowledge. More precisely, I will relate my reflections on Josip Broz Tito. It is to be expected that I will touch on the bases of his personality as much as of his politics.

My life was and is linked to Tito's. The strongest element in this account is Tito's own personality. Tito stands as one of the most complete, one of the most complex and enigmatic, of politicians. He will be seen thus, I think, not only in this age, and not only within the narrow confines of the Balkans.

Tito as a literary and political subject is magnified by the turbulent, meteoric course of his life. He was exceptional as an illustration of the link between a determined personality and a particular politics. He was a "political personality," and his private life engages us only in the context of his political disposition. Indeed, a literary study of the interlocking process by which Tito's personality was formed is both instructive and fascinating, particularly because he was a symbol of a national Communist rebellion and a national Communist heresy.

My search for the means by which that symbol was created leads me to sum up my knowledge of and my feelings about Tito. I do so not accidentally or indifferently. I am aware that while I have been writing the world has followed nervously—and Yugoslavs with distress—the dramatic course of Tito's final illness, his death, and its immediate aftermath.

Above all, my relationship with Tito is not over. We parted ideologically twenty-six years ago, yet for me all personal connections are not severed, though such is taken for granted within the Communist movement. I do not believe I owe him anything. What I did, I did out of my own convictions—and, in the last analysis, for my own sake. But I must admit that it was from Tito that I learned most about politics, not, to be sure, as one of the faithful, or even as his pupil. Through Tito, I discovered the essence of politics and political life. But I had opposing visions and aspirations. I sought an open society, personal freedom, and economic and political pluralism. I yearned for the power of law, not the law of power.

This can be defined, with qualification, as a form of negative instruction. Such instruction—the mutation and restructuring of what we know of Tito—can be the basis for movement and growth. Yugoslavia after Tito can be important in our time.

Historical events, and the role of historical personalities, teach us mainly, if not perhaps primarily, how not to act. Acting and creation cannot be taught literally. To say this does not diminish the significance of historical events and personalities; none of it will diminish Tito, or the events in which he played so decisive a role. Life and politics are irrepressible, ever new, re-created, only if they exert the will to resist rot and not fall into decay.

Such negative instruction is magical. That is what Tito taught me—though I became aware of it gradually only after my break with him. At that time, the end of 1953 and the beginning of 1954, I knew quite consciously and self-consciously that I had to break with him and his party. The alternative was to become faceless, to be bleached in the brilliance of his power. And I do not doubt that my obsession with my personal destiny obscured from me the reality of Tito's political personality and how much I had learned from him.

2

Josip Broz Tito was conspicuously without a particular talent except one—political. He had an exceptionally sharp and quick intelligence and a powerful and selective concentration. I observed similar characteristics in Stalin. Yet Stalin's thinking was more incisive—if somewhat slower—and showed a more acute and encompassing penetration.

Tito's qualities were manifested in both the security of his logic and the clarity of his purpose. When something was unclear to him, when he had not thought through something, he expressed himself with caution—even with confusion. That happened rarely and usually in unforeseen circumstances. His thinking so far outpaced his speech that on public occasions he would blur two or three sentences into one, with stuttering and hesitation.

Tito was in fact a poor speaker, but he could not bring himself to restrict, let alone forgo, opportunities for public appearance. The writer Radovan Zogović, while still a high Communist Party official, once remarked in jest that Tito would die if he were denied the chance to speak. In fact, it was through frequent interviews and speeches that Tito did his job; through them, he reacted to events and initiated changes, thereby enhancing his personal prestige and confirming his role as an indispensable leader. While it is true that the Party supported him in this role, and everyone acknowledged him as a charismatic figure, Tito himself was always aware of his role and persisted in it shrewdly, making it seem innate.

But Tito knew how to speak effectively when the issue was concrete and sharply defined, particularly in the case of internal Party disagreements. His speech in opposition to Marko Nikezić's attempt to expand the liberal trend in the Serbian Party (delivered at an impromptu forum of Serbian Communists in 1972) serves as a model of organization, of balanced and skillful persuasion. He was at his worst in those public ceremonies when he had to report on domestic or foreign affairs. Much the same could be said of Tito's writings: his official reports were too long and plainly awkward, while his articles on well-defined issues were shapely, lucid, direct.

Tito's education was inadequate. It could hardly have been otherwise, given his meager schooling, his limited training as a locksmith's apprentice. Yet he knew much more than a haphazard education gave to him. Among all the worker Communists that I ran across in prison—and among illegal revolutionaries there were many who were very clever—Tito stood out for the breadth of his knowledge, his swift comprehension. He seemed to know something about everything, although he suffered inwardly because he knew little of literature, art, and philosophy.

He also suffered because of his mutilated finger; the tip of the index finger on his left hand was caught in a machine when he worked as a mechanic. It was as if he bore the mark that he had not risen above the level of a worker. Only when it was politically advantageous would he allude to his origins as a workingman. Even when an underground operative, he dressed like a dandy, and when he joined a mountain-climbing club in 1934, he listed his occupation as an electrician. His forged identity papers described him as an engineer.

His skill was considerable in general technical matters, not just in a craft like locksmithing. In Siberia, convalescing as a war prisoner at the end of World War I, he operated a steam-powered mill. In Lepoglava, Croatia, where he was in prison in the early nineteen-thirties, he ran the power plant. While visiting factories with him, I noticed that no machine or mechanical process was alien to him, and novelties captured his special attention. He was familiar with agriculture and farm production. In the vineyard at Samobor—he acquired it with Party funds just before World War II, and expanded it after the war, adding a villa, in which he installed his brother—he would often explain to us in detail the wine-making process.

Yet he had superficial knowledge, nothing in depth except for the metalworking craft in which he had been trained—and of which he was somewhat ashamed. Even his knowledge of Marxism was meager. He knew the major works of Marx and Engels, Lenin and Stalin, and bits and pieces of economic theory and history. He had picked up the "classics of Marxism" randomly—in prison, in Moscow Party schools, which were rote sessions in which everyone declared his loyalty. I have been told, though, that in prison Tito was a conscientious and bright "student."

After the war, as I know, he was not an avid reader, though, to be fair, he had little time. He would scan the headlines and glance at the news stories. But he carefully read cables, reports, and bulletins of the Tanjug news agency. He was as uninterested in fiction as he was interested in those who wrote it.

He liked to play the piano, and went so far as to learn a few simple pieces. In his youth, he had regarded playing the piano as a mark of cultural prestige. At the height of his power, he saw it as another aspect of his special role. He danced nicely—a bit stiff, but elegantly—usually an old-fashioned waltz.

Obviously, Tito learned languages easily. After the war—or, rather, after the 1948 conflict with the Soviet Union—he mastered English well enough to be able to follow and grasp the simpler political texts. He had learned Russian as a prisoner during World War I, although it was apparent that he had never studied it thoroughly. He confused Serbian and Russian words that had the same pronunciation but different meanings. Still, his accent and pronunciation were more than adequate. He had a good ear and a strong memory. His French was poor, even though he had spent considerable time in Paris (preoccupied with Party activities). I believe that German was the foreign language in which he was most at home. I heard him converse in German—but my own poor command of German disqualifies me from evaluating his own.

On balance, he expressed himself worst in Serbo-Croatian. Here, his biggest mistake was to confuse idioms of Croatian origin with their Serbian counterparts. Further, his pronunciation inclined toward the dialect of Zagorje, his native region. He frequently resorted to Russian idioms. His public addresses only gave credence to rumors that he was not "our man" but a Russian. And among intellectuals one heard that he had not bothered to learn Serbo-Croatian.

Even late in life he continued to learn easily, aided by his good memory. When I first met him in 1937, he still could not quite spell correctly, though his grammar was accurate and his composition organized and well structured. He willingly accepted suggestions for improvement—unless they affected the content. After the war—often with Zogović —I edited his speeches for Tanjug, carefully preserving their meaning. Tito realized that this was necessary, but he never permitted it to be done by someone he did not trust. I remember, too, another example of how quickly he learned: on a certain occasion after the war he used the phrase "sine qua non"—his usage was correct, but he mispronounced it. I pointed out the error. He never made it again.

Tito did not possess, in my judgment and experience, a major military talent. By this I mean a military talent in the strictest sense, the ability to make sudden and right decisions in combat, to instill confidence as a quintessential commander. In my own wartime memoirs, I have challenged both his military knowledge and his capabilities as a tactical commander. That view was widely shared by our best military leaders, and Tito felt it. In a speech delivered in 1978 on the Neretva River, he polemicized against this view and indirectly against me by emphasizing that in Moscow from 1934 to 1935, following his prison term, he had been a rigorous student of military strategy.

Like most of Tito's statements, and those claims in semi-official biographies, this must be subjected to careful scrutiny. First of all, Tito stayed in Moscow for too short a time, and was too occupied with his Comintern activities, to have absorbed more than a cursory knowledge of the military sciences. Foreign students at the Moscow Party schools were, indeed, required to take courses in military tactics, but the instruction was general and superficial. Far more valuable was his experience during World War I as a noncommissioned officer in the Austro-Hungarian Army. This was reflected in his acceptance of the horrors of war, as well as in his highly developed sense of military organization and the realities of army life.

Whatever the range of his formal military knowledge, he had no talent as a military leader. He was oftentimes rash and nervous; he had an overwhelming concern for his personal safety; he sometimes issued contradictory orders. Oddly, he ordered major military units to be moved irrespective of the course of the battle.

Is this harsh? I think not. The three greatest and most decisive battles that were fought under his direct command reveal these shortcomings. They show the miscalculations and failed opportunities a steadier and more skillful commander in chief could have avoided.

Following the First Offensive in the fall of 1941, which culminated in the liquidation of what is known as the Republic of Užice (and the liberated territories in western and central Serbia), the chaos and the defeat were so overwhelming that Tito offered to resign as secretary of the Party. Certainly other elements contributed to this massive defeat, which led to the withdrawal of Supreme Headquarters from Serbia, with fewer than two thousand Partisans. There was at work, undoubtedly, left-wing agitation, an intensity of terror, and the remaining influence of "the old system." But the Supreme Commander's lack of resourcefulness and vision played a decisive role.

In the Fourth Offensive (Operation Weiss), and particularly in the critical battle on the Neretva in the early spring of 1943, Tito constantly changed his orders. His premature decision to destroy the bridge across the Neretva substantially impeded and complicated withdrawal. The situation was exceptionally difficult. In spite of blunders and erratic decisions, the battle was considered, by and large, a victory, but one that owed more to the ingenuity of his field commanders than to the Supreme Commander. In the Fifth Offensive (Operation Schwarz), Tito delayed his decisions, quite in contrast to his usual behavior. I was elsewhere at the time of that offensive, but I was told that Tito appeared lost, that he had a tendency to isolate himself with his retinue. It is a well-known fact—I have written about it elsewhere—that he was angry with those leaders who carried out the saving breakthrough without "waiting" for him.

His inadequacies as a military commander in these operations do not mean that Tito did not forcefully display his qualities as a political leader. The battle for Užice was a disaster, but the political and organizational activity of the Republic of Užice left an indelible imprint on our national experience. The Battle of Neretva inflicted a defeat on our chief internal enemies—the Chetniks of Draža Mihailović— from which they could never recover. It fortified the morale of Tito's new Partisan army and opened the way for Allied recognition of Tito and the new Yugoslavia. The Battle of Sutjeska was a triumph of the will of revolutionary forces over a modern army—and that will was, undoubtedly, a fusion of Tito's energy and spirit with the volatile rebelliousness of our people. Moreover, Tito recovered quickly from failure and weakness. Without much philosophizing and self-criticism, he learned his lesson and gained new knowledge. It was as if there were in him some indestructible rejuvenating force.

These qualities are not so much the qualities of a military commander, not primarily so, as they are those of a political leader. More precisely, they are qualities of a political leader in wartime. That is exactly what Tito was during the war—a glittering political talent. That talent was evident in the confidence with which he assessed the essential capacity of combat forces, in his ability to anticipate the action and counteraction in the course of war, and, above all, in his power to organize politically. Even in combat, Tito was highly concerned about his prestige and his authority. Indeed, his unprofessional and often rash leadership would certainly have undermined his reputation with Party officials and with military colleagues had they not perceived him as a decisive and cunning leader. He knew how to identify, at the right moment, the important and critical courses of action.

I remember Tito's countless tactical errors, his hasty reactions, his delayed decisions. But I remember, too, how clearly he grasped the character of that war. He saw it as a new form of power created through resistance to the occupation forces, as a means to and as a guarantee of victory through the transformation of guerrilla detachments into a regular army.

Still, I cannot recall, or now declare, that Tito made a single major or disastrous error save one: the leftist deviation in Serbia and Montenegro at the close of 1941 and the beginning of 1942, and for this other leaders were responsible as well. But Tito must be held accountable in his political function and through his endorsement by the Comintern. He was aware of that deviation, and he was quick to set the Party on the correct and victorious course.

His confusion and contradiction and vanity and conceit became secondary and were overlooked in a leader who confidently led his people to victory and to a new realm of brotherhood and freedom. His weaknesses and errors will not be remembered, while the glory of victory seems as assured as it was early on, when sacrifices were being made to it.

What is political talent? What was Tito's talent? Political talent is a personal quality that can be realized only within the context of broad social and national groups—and even then only within talented groups. The leader and the movement, the leader and the people, are symbiotic unions. One can speculate on this *ad infinitum;* the learned and the wise have already done so. Here, I dwell on Tito's qualities that are *not* characteristic of every politician, yet which enabled him to attain his exceptional and perhaps unprecedented success in politics.

These are: a strong sense of danger, as instinctive as it is rational; an unconquerable will to live, to survive, and to endure; a shrewd and insatiable drive for power. In Tito, these qualities were usually present, but their intensity fluctuated wildly: sometimes one impulse would lurk in obscurity, seemingly extinguished, only to flare up. I would say that in Tito all these became a single impulse, parts of which were expressed as necessity demanded. Is this the hallmark of all political leaders? I doubt it, but I am convinced that without this fusion of qualities there would have been no Tito and few of the deeds that are now linked to his name.

3

Tito was born a rebel. His character quickly perceived shifts in existing relationships; he constantly adjusted his own positions. From the beginning, he strove for something better than the craft to which his peasant origins and the poverty of a large family limited him. He changed jobs often, and upon induction into the Austrian Army in 1914, he was quickly accepted for training as a noncommissioned officer. Before that, as a worker, he had become a union member, automatically joining the Socialist Party. At the same time, nationalistic Croatian and then larger, Yugoslav, feelings began to stir within him. He did not engage in any substantial political activity, nor could he, for Yugoslav socialism was still in its infancy and only a handful of professional politicians and ideological theorists entertained the idea of a Yugoslav state.

In 1914, shortly after the outbreak of World War I, Tito was arrested. This occurred probably on a march to the Serbian front. He was jailed briefly—for a day—in Petrovaradin. Tito told Vladimir Dedijer that he had been arrested because he had, in a moment of anger, declared that he would surrender to the Russians. But according to Tito's own recent taped statement, he had been arrested as the result of a clerical error.

Subsequently, he was assigned to the Serbian front—a fact that until recently both he and his biographers kept hidden. Next he was dispatched to the Carpathian front to fight the Russians. As a noncommissioned officer he excelled in reconnaissance missions. Recently a letter was published in Austria saying that the Austrian command had cited noncommissioned officer Josef Broz for his courage on reconnaissance missions and in the taking of prisoners.

He was wounded and captured in the spring of 1915, but even then he did not join the volunteer detachment organized by Yugoslav prisoners in Russia. He remained in the camp, where he was almost flogged to death and then was locked up for leading a protest against the abuses of their Russian captors. After the February 1917 Revolution, he escaped from the camp and made his way to Petrograd. He participated in the July demonstrations, which, in the canon of Bolshevik history, are regarded as progressive. "I thought," Tito later said, "that the revolution was over, that it was finished."

He was expelled to the Urals, and escaped to Siberia, where he was at the time of the October Revolution. And it was there that he met his first wife, Pelagia Belousova. He joined the Communist Party in 1920, while still in Russia. In the same year he returned to his native land.

The period between 1920 and 1924 was the most inactive in Tito's political life. It was a period of disintegration and inactivity in the Yugoslav Communist Party, which had been banned and its leaders jailed. Tito became the father of three children, two of whom died in infancy. In spite of his political inactivity, Tito was dismissed from one job after another. In the following years he moved throughout Yugoslavia. In Bakar he was arrested. In Ogulin he was sentenced to prison for seven months, but a panel in Zagreb reduced the sentence to five months. He became active in trade unions, and at times was a salaried functionary. Early in 1928, he emerged in the front rank of the Party organization in Zagreb, as perhaps its most able representative, but he was not the *only* one, as the official historians maintain. The so-called Zagreb line was directed against factions of both the right and the left.

In August of 1928 he was again arrested and, at the so-called bomb-squad trial, was sentenced to five years in prison. At the trial he declared: "I do not feel guilty . . . because I do not consider this court competent to judge me . . . only the court of the Party can judge me." While that declaration proves his courage and loyalty to the Party, it also reflects the ritualistic conduct prescribed for Communists in the presence of the "class court." Tito's conduct before the court has been mythologized in Yugoslavia, though there were other Communists who conducted themselves similarly. Recorded history is just only toward its masters.

Official accounts cite the police as having planted the bombs on Tito. But this is curious! It is embarrassing to admit that Yugoslavia's later visionary leader was collecting weapons at a time when conditions were hardly ripe for an armed struggle. Yet Tito told me that he believed that conditions even in the prewar years could foster armed insurrection and revolution. I am doubtful. The royal police, however arrogant and brutal, planted nothing on anyone. The Kingdom of Yugoslavia was a corrupt and undemocratic state, but it was a state in which law exacted more respect, and the courts more independence, than they do today in Yugoslavia.

Tito served his first year in prison with dignity. He told me how he had disobeyed a guard's order to pick up cigarette butts. I heard nothing but praise for him from other Communists jailed with him. Within that select Communist environment, Tito was conspicuous for his spirit, his steadiness, his diligence in applying himself to the study of Marxism, and his intuitiveness. He also made an impression by his self-absorption and impenetrability.

Upon his release from prison at the end of 1934, Tito left for Vienna, and then for Moscow, at the direction of the Central Committee. The year 1935 was a year of purges in the Soviet Union. A new and decisive phase began in the revolutionary development of Josip Broz, who had gone through many painful trials but had yet to comprehend that revolutionary institutions and methods, though inseparable from the idea of revolution, are still more important than that idea.

A basic component of his personality was vigorous resistance to perceived reality. Josip Broz began from nothing, as nobody and nothing. From the start he did not accept the commonly perceived reality.

The surname Broz derives from Ambroz, and as a name dates back to the fifteenth century. But there is no evidence that Tito's family descended from the first generation of Brozes. According to Tito's family account, his ancestral Brozes migrated from the border region between Bosnia and Dalmatia to Zagorje, where they settled, probably in the sixteenth century. Before that, according to Tito, they had fled the Montenegrin tribe of Kuče.

The Broz clan was large, some of them cultivated persons, some prominent in Zagreb. But Tito's branch of the clan were peasants. Still, the house in which Tito was born on May 7, 1893, was among the finest in the town of Kumrovec. The family had to struggle to survive because of its large size—there were fifteen children, eight of whom died prematurely—and Tito's father's bad management of promissory notes. They did own land, eight acres near the town market—no small amount, even though the land was not choice. Tito's mother, Marija, came from a well-to-do Slovenian peasant family. Tito, who looked like his mother, spent much of his childhood with his maternal grandfather. None of his brothers or sisters led notable lives, in either success or failure. Tito owed his rise in life to no particular member of his family, although he allowed some members of his family to profit from his rise.

From the start, from early youth, Tito refused to accept the fate of being one among many. The war and the Russian Revolution, with Communism growing in both, were the forms and the realities, the dreams and the visions, through which he realized himself. In a peaceful, largely nonideological world, he would have been a union official or entrepreneur, an authoritarian father, a willful husband.

In the Communist messianic historical role of the working class, Tito found personal and sacrificial social meaning. Although he had no particular respect for the working class, he was staunch and unflagging in his interpretation of the worker's historical role. Whenever he used the phrases "the working class," "workers," "working people," it sounded as if he were talking about himself—about the aspirations of those in the lowest ranks of society to the glamour of government and the ecstasy of power.

In Communism, Tito found himself; and in Tito, Communism found a most successful, a most distinctive protagonist. I have known many a Communist who was ideologically more steadfast, but never have I known one who would assert, as did Tito, his own uniqueness and exclusiveness to such a degree and in such detail. His obsession with luxury, the pomp in Tito's character, grew all the more potent and elaborate as it fed on the consolidation of his personal power.

But singularity, whether real or simulated, does not preclude ostentation and vulgarity. Tito's appetite for luxury, for the fashionably acceptable, and his royal way of life and autocratic use of power were antiquated and degrading. He moderated himself only when he suspected that it might weaken his position and his prestige. Toward the end of 1949, while I was in New York at a session of the United Nations, *Life* magazine published an article about Tito with photographs of him in front of his villas, in his drawing rooms, flanked by his horses and dogs, surrounded by his inner circle, of which I was a part along with his son Žarko and others. It did not go unnoticed that Tito came off as a kind of Latin-American dictator.

At that time, Yugoslavia's popularity was increasing as a result of its resistance to Soviet hegemony. Our leadership was eager to present itself in a non-Soviet, democratic light. When we returned to Belgrade and convened to review our mission, I drew Tito's attention to the detrimental aspects of that kind of publicity, quoting the phrase "Latin-American dictator." Aleš Bebler, I believe, had used this phrase in New York. Tito blushed and fell silent. Yet nothing changed, except that, for a while, he was more circumspect around Western journalists.

In 1950 or 1951, when we discussed whether or not to dispose of the villas, the private lodges and spas that had been requisitioned for the personal use of Party leaders,

Tito's response was that he would give up his villa in Opatija, because it was so close to his official residence at Brioni that he didn't use it. Yet he continued to build villas and palaces for his exclusive use—even though he may not have spent more than a night in some of them.

In 1953, it was decided to allow towns, streets, factories, and cooperatives to revert to their old names—names that had been replaced by names of Party leaders. Tito went along, but it was agreed that he was exempt from that rule. Something similar happened with the relay race run on Tito's birthday. The denunciation of Stalin's cult of the personality at the Twentieth Congress of the Communist Party of the Soviet Union provoked similar responses in Yugoslavia. Tito suggested that the day of the race be designated the "Day of Youth" and no longer be associated with his birthday. But the celebration itself became even more gigantic, more popular—in line with Tito's vision of his charismatic role as a leader in relation to the impersonal, monolithic masses.

Tito jealously guarded everything that touched on his personality. Whoever questioned his style, or infringed on his prerogatives, risked his anger, if not worse, that is, the label of hostility and anti-Partyism. This attitude sprang from his personality: always and in everything, Tito cared most intensely about his dignity, his singularity. Never, not even during the war, in mountain bivouacs or on night marches, did I come upon him in an unseemly posture or hear him speak coarsely. He was always clean-shaven, neat, and organized, as if invulnerable to the conditions of war.

Everything that was his—his horse, his clothes, his weapons—had to be superior. His comrades, too, made sure with a certain tenderness that he was happy and comfortable. The consolidation of his power and his role ran parallel to his inborn sense of superiority and his conviction that he deserved special care. But in the end autocratic power transformed proud and decent impulses into self-serving and undemocratic ones, and his closest and most faithful comrades became both leaders and toadies.

Personalities make an imprint on their time and their society in proportion to their spiritual power and creative skill. The more independent a nation is of its leaders, the more creative it is. Everyone loses in identifying leaders with nations and history, for life must have fresh vistas and open streams. Tito did not quite understand that: he built himself up into something above and beyond the people and the movement. That "grandeur" will be taken from him because it is not his. But he will survive as a historical figure, politically gifted and in many ways creative.

4

Although Tito strove to identify himself with historic events, he did not succumb to uncontrolled anger or frenzied violence. During the war, his concern for the safety of his people—his "cadres"—was marked, even though his concern for his own safety was still greater. Indeed, that concern seemed to grow in proportion to the duration of his position and the extent of his power. This was not solely a matter of emotion. He felt a responsibility for the Party and for the uprising. What would happen if he were killed? He identified his personal power with the revolutionary transformation.

No matter how Tito's wartime role is interpreted, there can be no doubt that he was urgently aware of danger to his army. During the Fourth Offensive, at the beginning of 1943, when the area around the Rama and the Neretva was encircled, he repeatedly changed his orders, sometimes issuing commands that were ambiguous. But at the same time, dangerously, courageously, and selflessly, he carried out a regrouping of troops that insured the rescue of the wounded and defeated the Germans at Vilica Guvno. He managed

to release the Partisans from their "German complex"—
their obsessive belief in the innate superiority of the German armed forces. Tito on the Neretva was a tiger in a
cage, clawing about for weak spots—among the Italians and
the Chetniks, of course—gouging out a hole wide enough
for the Partisan storm to gush through. In May of 1943,
at the beginning of the Fifth Offensive, he said: "We have
never been in such danger!" Others felt that danger, too,
but less intensely, and were slower to undertake defensive
measures for our safety.

There were battles when hours counted, even minutes:
the breakthrough of the Second Proletarian Brigade at
Vučevo, in the Piva Canyon, before the Germans blocked
the way out; the recapture of Ljuba's Grave by the Fourth
Montenegrin Brigade; the decisive and self-initiated breakthrough by the First Proletarian Brigade. Tito's personal
role as commander in these clashes was insignificant, perhaps negligible. But it was he who imposed a sense of
danger, who established a momentum, who forced the tide
to turn.

Tito's personality thrived on the heat of the moment,
yielding readily, instinctively, to fresh impressions, but
was far too rash in situations of unexpected or drastic
change. People like Tito do not always weigh things or
think them through. They blend frenzy and fortitude, exactitude and recklessness. He had another side—intense,
cautious, capable of assessing complex major issues and
decisive moves. All action that lies between these two poles
—between the deliberate and the impulsive, the momentary
and the far-reaching—was not typical of Tito, though he,
like all of us, lived and acted within a mostly banal, everyday routine. After all, life *is* largely a banal, everyday routine.

It would be a delusion to think that one was dealing with two personalities, however. I saw the nervous, quick-tempered Tito as only a preparation—a warm-up, even a purgatory—for that other, deliberate, masterful, resolute, Tito. Indeed, in crucial political decision-making Tito was extraordinarily bold. He was also infallible—if we equate being infallible with being successful.

In 1937, at the time of the Soviet purges, the Comintern designated Tito as the head of the Yugoslav Communist Party. It was after Milan Gorkić, the Secretary of the Party, had been arrested and Yugoslav emigration to the U.S.S.R. had been reduced. Of course, he could not have been appointed to that position, with the right to veto all decisions (the right that would ease his rise through the ranks of the Party, although the Party was Stalinized by then, both ideologically and in its cadres), had he not been personally checked out, his loyalty to the Soviet leadership tested, or, rather, his disloyalty to the factionalists within his own party confirmed. Many other Communists had been checked out in that same fashion and they had not survived.

Later, Tito said of that time: "I made no friends among the factionalists, I minded my own business, and I was careful about what I said, particularly in rooms with telephones." Tito was the only leader who groped his way through the horror of the security checks and the liquidations. And he did so, to all appearances, in a direct and simple manner. He sensed danger, but at the same time he steadfastly believed in the Soviet course. He had an instinct for danger, and experience taught him how power shapes the destiny of the movement and the idea. I remember Tito returning from Moscow, from the first socialist state, exhausted and upset, seeking relief and encouragement among his underground comrades in "military fascistic," "monarchic-fascistic" Yugoslavia.

Did Tito buy his absolution through betrayal, through slandering his comrades? What really was Tito's role in the great purges, specifically within the Yugoslav Party? Of course, words and ideas are not immutable and do not live or retain a lasting sense independent of the social and spiritual climate. That is particularly true of the language of politics, as George Orwell knew.

Here, we must look at the Soviet experience. Collaboration with Soviet intelligence in the prewar period (and even today, somewhere, and for someone) was (and is) regarded as an honor worthy of recognition. Soviet agents commanded extraordinary powers of secrecy and force. In Europe, Communists dreamed, so to speak, of the bliss of performing sublime service for the Soviet Union. In different circumstances and altered relationships, even for Communists this sublime service could become a source of shame and betrayal. Under Lenin, loyalty to the Soviet Union had become synonymous with being a Communist and a revolutionary. Under Stalin, the society's goals called for loyalty to Stalin. Even before the Great Terror, the followers of Trotsky, rightists, and other deviants—all the willful and the unwitting—had been anathematized and many of them arrested.

Tito became secretary of his party in 1937 in the midst of this most deranged mass terror. For quite some time, he had been loyal to Stalin. It was irrelevant for him as well as for many others that Stalin was Lenin's most legitimate heir, because it became a matter of being loyal to specific Stalinist policy, of acquiescing in Stalin's methods. It should not be forgotten that as far back as 1928, Josip Broz was one of the most outspoken adversaries of factionalism and one of the most prominent supporters of the monolithic character of the Party. In Party practice, that means the total sovereignty, within the Party, of one's own line was, at root, Stalinist.

Josip Broz supported Stalin and Stalin's monolithic policies—in short, Stalin's Soviet Union—long before his arrival in the U.S.S.R. early in 1935. Moreover, he was a prototype —not the only one, but one of the most resourceful and most adroit—of the new monolithic and monopolistic spirit within the Party. Stalin and Stalinism were compatible with Tito's mentality and with the extent of his ideological development. He himself energetically purged his own party; the participation of the Yugoslav Communists in the Moscow purges had been for him logical and inevitable. Why feel guilty when one is advancing Bolshevism, forging and consolidating the party that would clear the way for him to the ideal and to power.

I remember Tito and Edvard Kardelj (as former "Muscovites," they had known most of the Yugoslavs arrested in the Soviet Union) saying that Soviet authorities had relieved us of the burden of "factionalism." How grotesque it is today to hear Stane Dolanc and other younger men in Tito's entourage attempting to prove that even before the war, and right in the middle of Moscow, Tito had already begun his struggle against Stalin and Stalinism! If Tito had not been loyal to the Soviet Union—which is to say, Stalin— how could he have survived? How could he, for that matter, have concealed his motives from those of us who were Stalinists in his own country, Stalinists who had never even seen Moscow? Moscow designated an authentic personality to head an authentically Stalinist, or, rather, Leninist, Party.

Yet it is my impression and my conviction that Tito's

participation in the purges was limited; they were, for him, secondary. Moscow was so disenchanted with the Yugoslav Party that it almost disbanded it, as it had the Party in Poland. In the Comintern, Tito was distrusted by the chief of the "cadres," a Bulgarian. The periodic reports that Tito, as secretary of the Party, was required to submit, giving information on the behavior of his fellow Yugoslavs, were written after the fact. These reports were usually negative, because those on whom he reported had already been arrested by the NKVD, or had been denounced by underground agents as enemies. In *Proleter,* the organ of the Central Committee, Tito automatically justified the expulsion and the arrest of the factionalists by labeling them with epithets borrowed from capital cases, not subject to appeal or review: Trotskyites, traitors, factionalists, spies, antiparty elements, and so forth.

Even in Yugoslavia, the purges in the Party were merciless. But their standard-bearer was not Tito; he was out of the country most of the time. The new generation, absorbed in revolutionary activity, was either unaware of the sufferings of political victims in the U.S.S.R. or quick to overlook them. When he was in Yugoslavia, Tito was undertaking responsible work, although he maintained connections with Moscow and Soviet intelligence, ties about which other members of the Politburo speculated, and about which they knew nothing except what Tito told them. I maintain that he did not have much to conceal. In reality, Tito began gradually to elude Soviet control. It cheered him when, after he returned from Moscow in 1939, we told him that we had made the Party financially self-sustaining. That, our first, financial independence was far more important than it seemed at the time.

With the outbreak of World War II, and of the revolution, political differences began to emerge, political differences between a new superpower and a small country. Tito had difficulty finding a common language with Moscow. He sought the advice of the Comintern, but also made decisions by himself (or in concert with his comrades) on critical issues. At the second session of the AVNOJ (the Partisan assembly), held at Jajce on November 29, 1943, the most important decisions were made without Moscow's knowledge, and provoked Soviet objections: Yugoslavia was made into a federal state; the monarchy was effectively abolished; and the revolutionary government, with the Communists at its helm, was legalized.

The strengthening of Tito's role ran parallel to the consolidation of the revolution, and therefore to his influence in Moscow. Moscow was caught in its own trap: the Soviet hierarchy, committed ever more irrationally to fostering the "cult" of its leader, was in no position to resist Tito's increasing strength, which derived from the revolutionary process and strategic propaganda. Moreover, Yugoslavia was an independent state. The cult of Tito, which in one of its aspects imitated the cult of Stalin, would, as the impending conflict with the Soviet Union came to a head, serve to strengthen Yugoslavia's capacity for independent resistance.

Someone might observe—and not without reason—that a democratic Yugoslavia would have resisted Soviet control without the cult of Tito, by virtue of its social structure. But Yugoslavia had already been transformed into an authoritarian and autocratic Communist state. Except for the Communists, there were no effective political forces. Soviet claims could have been countered by methods and approaches similar to those of the Soviets themselves. Under the circumstances, only a Leninist, or, rather, a Stalinist,

party with a legacy of successful revolution could successfully resist Moscow's authority.

How did Tito take the conflict with the Soviet Union in
1948? How large and how important a role did he play in
it? For Tito, the break with Moscow, however gradual, came
as a bitter psychological and intellectual blow. It was the
opinion of those close to him, and he himself believed, that
the period marked the onset of his gall-bladder attacks. In
public and in the presence of strangers, particularly the
Soviet Embassy staff, if he had to receive them, he acted with
composure and self-confidence. He was successful at that
because he was a gifted political performer. But Soviet intelligence, which had posted its agents around him, knew
better, and with those close to him Tito did not conceal
what he was going through.

In those months he was fretful, easily agitated, and broke
out suddenly into expressions of intimacy and warmth toward his closest and most trusted comrades—an intimacy and
warmth he had lost toward the end of the war and in the
early postwar years. True, he did not then have the support
of today's "half-established" institutions, though he had the
steady, and secretly reluctant, support of Moscow.

That is why I look back on that period—the end of the
war and the two or three years following it—as barren and
somehow undignified. From a hopeful writer and revolutionary, I saw myself transformed by victory into the instrument of propaganda for an even more absolute monarch
than King Alexander had been, and the spokesman for a
failed and obviously unjust social order. I wanted to return
to writing, to retreat into literature. I even discussed this
with Tito. He agreed that I should schedule my time somehow or other to include both my writing and my official

propaganda activities. But presentiments of the gathering conflict with Moscow unleashed in me new impulses—hope for something new together with a heightened sense of service to the country and the Party.

Though Tito was torn psychologically over the split with Moscow, he did not falter, and indeed strengthened the independence of his government. Surely, his scathing and flustered reactions—characteristic of him in thorny situations—during the clash with the Soviet leadership were intensified by his former obligations to Moscow. His concern was, above all, for the future of Yugoslavia, his own creation. With good reason, Tito felt the pressure of the past, and, even more implacably, the stress of the present.

He recognized the risks. Significantly, later (perhaps in 1949) he said of those Yugoslav leaders who had been "purged" in the Soviet Union: "They should have been hit over the head, but not beheaded." During the crisis of June 1948, while in the park of the Kranj palace drafting the reply declining participation in the Cominform session at Bucharest—during which we were to be subjected to an "ideological" trial—Tito burst out in anger: "If we have to be killed, we'll be killed on our own soil!" In this, he was surely not alone, but, as the man at the top, he was more forceful than most. The politician who makes no sacrifice for his actions is not a politician, though of course the actions may not merit the sacrifice.

In and out of the Central Committee, there were Communists no less bold than Tito during the conflict with Moscow. But Tito's role was the most decisive, given his power and prestige. Even without him, however, there would have been resistance, the conflict would have erupted; and I believe that it would have been successful. But if Tito had bowed to Moscow, chaos and demoralization would have been inevitable. That he could not accept: he knew and understood too well the essence of Bolshevik power— and of Stalin himself—to be unaware of what would be in store for him.

There was one thread in the pattern of those days that was personal, which with Tito could never quite be divorced from the political. The other thread was to defend and preserve Yugoslavia and her government's authority. His personal fate became identified with his personal power —an absolute power—and all was determined in that moment of concurrence, challenged only by the pro-Soviet minority in the Party. Courage and endurance in the contest with Moscow were Tito's duty, his personal destiny, and his historical mission.

Probably because of that blend of the personal and the objective, of private danger and historical role, Tito displayed a unique characteristic: his own brand of intuitive pragmatism. Immediately after the split with Moscow, he sensed the strength of Yugoslavia's international position: an attack on that country, on Yugoslavia, would provoke international complications, quite apart from the already potentially explosive "cold war."

Tito was not at his best in abstract ideological disputes. When the conflict with the Soviets came to a boil and threatened gravely to undermine our Party ideology, Kardelj and I had to convince him that without an ideological squaring of accounts with the Soviet system, without ideological backing for our positions, we would lose our bearings, our confidence, and our stability.

Within the narrow corridors of power at the top, there were no differences regarding the question of Soviet pressure. But from the start, there were nuances in our points of view. The "theoretical" group—Edvard Kardelj, Boris

Kidrič, Vladimir Bakarić, myself, and others—favored an extension of the struggle into the realm of theory. For us, the conflict expressed a crisis in Leninism, in the Soviet form of socialism. Tito, Alexander-Leka Ranković and the "pragmatists" favored confining the struggle to the sphere of power and the state. At the beginning, we all blazed away, and we all racked our brains. Sometimes, I thought I saw heads bursting the armor of inherited, automatically absorbed dogma!

But this division into two "schools" does not explain Tito's diatribe against me and against several others un-named, which was voiced recently, so many years after my break with him. He accused us of having omitted part of his reply to the Molotov-Stalin letter of March 27, 1948. In that portion of his letter, Tito outlined, accurately and succinctly, what the relationship should be among socialist countries. He submitted the text to us before the meeting of the Politburo—a sign of the altered atmosphere and the shift in his own attitude, because prior to that he had never done anything like it. Someone—I think it was I—observed that that portion of the letter would particularly infuriate the Soviet leadership because it impinged on ideology, over which they claimed authority. Kardelj, Ranković, and others present agreed, and they suggested that I men-tion it to Tito. I did so at my meeting with him. He accepted my advice unequivocally.

It was shortly after 1949 that our separate schools of thought, the theoretical and the pragmatical, merged into one. Tito accepted ideological innovations, only to retract them after Stalin's death, because he saw them as political ballast and a threat to his personal power.

Even though he was deeply shaken by the confrontation with Moscow, Tito himself set the stage for that confrontation. Of course, he was not alone in the staging of the conflict, or the most radical protagonist. Yugoslav relations with Moscow followed a zigzag pattern until the time when Soviet designs for economic and political domination became overt. In line with our judgment and the circumstances, we never relinquished our authority and our integrity. Little by little, from the small ring of power at the top to the broader circles below, we began to rebuke the Soviet system and criticize Soviet policy toward us and, by extension, toward much of the rest of Eastern Europe as well. In all of this, certainly within his inner circle, Tito was cautious but persistent. He was ever mindful of the danger his course of action posed to himself and to Yugoslavia.

It was an agonizing passage through dogma and reality—the dogma and reality of yesterday, but nonetheless our own. Tito was not hindered by all that pain and internal turbulence. On the contrary, it inspired him to further boldness and resourcefulness. In that struggle with Moscow, in those reverberations of thought and emotion, there were blunders and excesses, particularly the persistent attempt, for which Tito was largely responsible, to extricate Albania from Soviet influence and subjugate it to Yugoslavia. Stalin and the Soviet government took these imbalanced and hegemonic Yugoslav designs on Albania as a pretext to launch attacks on Yugoslavia, and to subjugate further the Eastern European countries. Tito's aggression toward Albania was both an imitation of Soviet methods and one of his ways of protecting himself against them. But in the face of Soviet and Albanian resistance, he wisely retreated on this front.

The resistance of Yugoslav Communism to Soviet expansionism would have yielded far more significant and extensive results had the leadership broadened ideological differences, and had the leader been less susceptible to the magic of power. But history and political struggles and political relations do not choose leaders; leaders choose them. Tito's need for identification with history, with the deed in which he played the most pivotal role, was at once his strength and his weakness. He had a courageous, selfless feeling for the historical moment. But he also restricted the flow of life, limited civil rights, and manipulated men and nations.

5

It can be convincingly demonstrated from Marxist doctrine
(or other Communist doctrine) that no single Communist
leader is in fact a true Communist. At best, he is only a
half-Communist. Such a scrutiny of purity would spare not
even Lenin, to say nothing of Marx and Engels themselves.
How could we reconcile with Communist internationalism
Lenin's acceptance of financial aid from the German high
command and his signing of a peace treaty with the Kaiser's
generals at Brest-Litovsk—almost the day after Lenin assumed power? As we all know, Engels was an industrialist
with aristocratic manners. Marx speculated in the stock
market and, in denouncing his rivals, he was a precursor of
Stalin's school. Of Stalin, I must here observe that, by
reliable statistical account, he exterminated approximately
seven hundred thousand Communists, to say nothing of
millions of others. This death toll of Communists was more
than was caused by the entire range of reactionary powers,
put together, since the introduction of scientific socialism.

The gulf between political philosophy and political practice is inevitable; the more political philosophy aspires to be

scientific and infallible, the deeper that gulf. A similar phenomenon occurred in the sphere of religion during preindustrial epochs: ecclesiastical dignitaries were rarely the object lessons of their sermons, and rulers far too often enforced their orthodoxy by massacre and pillage. No political teaching—since it is finally only the spiritual and logical distillation of given realities—can transcend the homogeneous nature and the structural model of consciousness. Nor can it by itself act as an agent to direct and mobilize certain social groups, for life-giving forces grow from manifold and unpredictable elements. Therefore, Communist leaders should not be faulted more than other leaders for their lack of consistency and even their want of principle—except that Communists suppress such evidence, and they stifle the birth of new visions by intolerance and force.

If Tito were to be subjected to doctrinal Communist scrutiny, he would stand condemned—as one of the most inconsistent and least Communist of rulers—more because of his royal way of life than for his autocratic way of governing. On the other hand, though many Communists will not remember Tito kindly, his name cannot evoke the horror and condemnation of Stalin's. That conviction— though it may be colored by my past and my association with Tito—I rest as much on an analysis of Communist autocrats as I do on an analysis of other revolutionary autocrats. Not for nothing did one of my friends say of Communism: the more faulty and inconsistent the better.

However, this should not lead us to the conclusion that Tito was essentially different from or better or worse than other Communist leaders more or less committed to the ideology of Marx and Lenin. To put it simply: he accommodated himself to existing conditions. It is known how brutally, and with what little regard for mitigating circumstances, the counterrevolutionary rivals were treated in the aftermath of victory. In the summer of 1946, while I was driving to Bled and Ljubljana with an official of the Polish Ministry of Foreign Affairs—a man far too young for such a high position, but a strict Communist—he told me how Stalin had reprimanded the Polish delegation for the tepid measures they had adopted toward their opponents. In contrast, Stalin had praised Tito: "Tito is a tower of strength . . . he wiped them all out!" I recounted the story to my comrades in the Central Committee, and we felt a cruel but not unpleasant pride. I am saying all this not to denounce anyone, or to justify myself (I was in some things worse, in some things better, than others); I offer it only as a historical fact and a lesson for the future.

We know the destructive results of ideological anti-Stalinist collectivization designed to prove that Stalin was wrong in his accusations regarding the kulak policy of the Yugoslav Party. We know of the oppressive, still-frustrated Zhdanovian methods in ideological and cultural areas; for those methods, according to official and semiofficial sources, I alone am responsible, even thirty years later. And just as we were appalled, after 1948, by Stalin's denunciations and aggressions, so, before that, we had basked in the glow of his approval. Politics cannot be grasped or interpreted outside of the totality of specific circumstances.

But Tito's deviation from the purity of Communist doctrine—rather like that of Stalin and Mao—affirms more than it refutes his steady and unflagging adherence to Marxism and socialism, or, rather, to Lenin's variation of Communism. What did the ideology of Marx and Lenin mean to Tito? What did he see as essential, unchangeable, inviolate in that ideology?

From his personal experience of the Russian Revolution,

as well as from his exposure to its propaganda, he must have learned that revolution and new forms of power could not be realized or survive without the support of a new kind of party. He must have seen that such a party must be centralized in its ideology as well as in its organization. Upon his return from Russia as a released prisoner of war, that knowledge was to be tested, clarified, and forged in the crucible of the vagaries of the Yugoslav Party. By nature, Tito was a man of action: words, speeches, meetings were alien to him, even intolerable—unless they served as an instrument of political action. As a Party and union activist, he perceived not only the futility, but also the destructiveness, of factions for the Party. The Party should, he felt, integrate consciousness and the class struggle in its progress toward revolutionary dictatorship.

Until 1928, he leaned to the left. His own experience and the shared experience of the young activists drawn from the lower rungs of the Party—and the initiative of the Comintern against national factions ("An Open Letter to the Members of the Communist Party of Yugoslavia" in 1928) —confirmed Tito's vision of a party free of factions, one active among the masses. That is, in embryo, a variation of Stalin's variation of the Leninist Party, for the ideological integrity of the Party was Stalin's invention, and in due time it was realized in the Party leader's monopoly of ideology. For Tito, ideological integrity was a given, a *fait accompli,* the unequivocal, religious acceptance of Leninism and the Soviet Party as the model. The Party had merely to be purged of factions, and the most reliable way—indeed, the way to insure this—was through unremitting actions under a monolithic leadership.

Once the concept of such a party, and such leadership, is defined, it becomes an *a priori* truth. His five years in prison

denied Tito the opportunity to organize and consolidate
such a party, not counting his small group of fellow prisoners. But the January 6, 1929, proclamation of a dictatorship by King Alexander unleashed a tide of new, young
Communists—free of the past, free of factions—who would
take both Leninism and the Party shaped by Lenin and
Stalin for granted as the only possible model for revolutionary practice. That was the atmosphere and reality Tito
encountered upon his release from prison in 1934. In Moscow he encountered terror mobilized in the name of ideological unity and the classless society. What for Yugoslavs
was the revolutionary ideal was in the U.S.S.R. already the
terror of the privileged class. When, in 1937, Tito was
chosen by the Comintern for the leadership of the Yugoslav
Communist Party, shortly after his stay in Moscow and the
arrest of its former secretary, Milan Gorkić, the Party in
Yugoslavia was already Bolshevized, unswervingly loyal to
the Soviet Union and to Stalin, and under the leadership
of the uncompromising and militant ranks consolidated by
the January 6 dictatorship.

When my generation entered the revolutionary struggle
and the Party in the early thirties, everything was uncon-
ditionally accepted—Leninism, the Comintern, the Soviet
Union, and, in the mid-thirties, even Stalin, despite the
purges and the trials. In truth, we knew less than we believed we did. But for revolutionary action, that is not
necessarily a drawback; it may even be advantageous. Tito
understood all that and aligned himself with those new
ranks—one of the very few from the older generation to do
so. That was the Party he had wanted, for which he had
fought and slaved in prison, and he was to rise, as he deserved, to its leadership. His leadership would be personal,
dictatorial, the kind of leadership which at that time only

Moscow had the power to award or to deny. He was not going to fritter away authority, because, for one thing, it was not in the interest of Moscow. Moreover, dissent at home and duplicity in Moscow had taught him that in politics, particularly in Communist politics, the relationship of power and interest is paramount. Without power in his own country, it was impossible to survive in the domain of Soviet ideological tyranny.

It is simply because of this early coda that the ideology of Marx and Lenin remained for Tito until the very end essential, unchangeable, and inviolate. That ideology presupposes not only a Bolshevik Communist Party, but also a leader (at least a leadership) who will direct the Party and preserve its ideological purity. Ideology and the Party are vitally linked. Ideology must not alter its basis. The Party must wage a continuous struggle in pursuit of its monopolistic power. Together, these form a process that must go on until the utopian future is achieved, a future in which there will be no class systems, no power, and no politics.

It is obvious that such power cannot exist without a utopian ideology. Not only did Tito learn and adopt this truth, but he also absorbed it consciously as a condition and instrument of his personal ascent and his personal fate. For him, ideology and theory were inseparable from politics. True, he did not reduce ideology to a means of power—which is characteristic of Soviet leadership. But he did not separate power from ideology: ideological consciousness was for him the other side of the coin of power. He showed a certain flexibility and liberalism occasionally in theoretical disputes, but he did not let this go beyond constructive criticism—let alone criticism of the dictatorship of the proletariat, which is to say, of the Party's control of power. Because relations within the Party insured Tito's personal power, he considered any intimation of revision of Lenin's postulations about such power a threat to his personal role. During the period of the confrontation with Stalin, whenever doubts were expressed about the socialist character of the Soviet Union and an analogy was made with Yugoslavia, Tito felt not only that his country was threatened but also that he was himself insulted. I thought of him sometimes as a kind of high priest embittered by heresy.

The basic elements of this ideology—materialism and materialistic dialectics, history as the class struggle, the inevitability of socialism in the world, the avant-garde role of the Party in the realization of the classless society—could no more be altered than Tito's own prestige and position. In January of 1954, in connection with my case of criticizing the society, when I was summoned before Tito in the presence of Ranković and Kardelj, I observed at some point that I had concluded that Engels was wrong to introduce dialectics into nature. Defensively Tito asked me: "Are you ready to announce that publicly?" I replied, with a pathetic naïveté: "Always—and gladly!" It never came to that, of course, because soon—on the basis of Kardelj's report delivered at the Plenum of the Central Committee—I was denounced for "revisionism," and Tito interpreted my views as the emergence of a class enemy in the Party. The point is this: the confrontation with Stalin had revealed the probability of wars between the Communist states, but it had not signaled a change in the power and ideology of those states.

Is it possible to change (or develop) Marxism, Leninism, and not undermine the socialist foundations on which political party and government rest? It was Bakunin, with the intuition of an anarchic utopian, who observed first that Marx's doctrines lead inevitably toward the creation of monstrous, oppressive state machinery. It was demonstrated, in Bakunin's very homeland, that indeed such a monstrous machinery can be realized. It is not accidental that Lenin took from Marxism his basic doctrine about power: the dictatorship of the proletariat.

Whether power is, in fact, the dictatorship of the proletariat is totally irrelevant from the political point of view. But it is important that Lenin extracted that concept from Marxism and applied it to Russian conditions. The concept of Marxism as a fundamental spiritual force which is not exclusively concerned with power exists today only in certain Western universities. In Communist countries, there is no Marxism except its Leninist variant: prescribed behavior, a fearsome opium of consciousness, the obligatory element of power.

Tito's Marxism does not differ from Marxism in other Communist countries in function—the sanctification and entrenchment of power—but by its Yugoslav character, by its insistence on the independence of the state and its models. Tito's pragmatic Leninism, together with Kardelj's blend of social and democratic verbalism, and the notion of Leninistic Party monopoly are merging gradually into a Yugoslav variant of Marxist authoritarianism. An independent and monopolistic power still demands an unerring ideology.

The foundations of ideology and consequently of power thus remain intact while they grow and improve. Tito was not—nor had he any reason to be—categorically opposed to such theorizing, although he accepted it only *a posteriori*. He quickly understood after his break with the U.S.S.R. that dictatorial power, especially in a small and undeveloped country, stagnates and rots if it ceases to inspire the social structure on which it rests.

Bold and imaginative in practice, Tito was cautious, overly cautious, in making political decisions, let alone in inventing ideas. Not one of the great ideas of Yugoslav Communism is his.

I conceived the idea of self-government in 1950. It was later elaborated by Kidrič and Kardelj. Now they say—although I have no desire to vie for credit—that self-government was already in effect during the revolution! Moreover, at first Tito resisted self-government—only later to accept it in its simplified, practical form. (Ah, I see what it is—factories to the workers!) Nor did our differentiation from the Bolshevik, Leninistic kind of Party originate with him—a differentiation that was expressed in our renaming the Communist Party the "League of Communists." This decision, enacted by the Sixth Congress in 1952, relatively nondogmatic and non-Leninist, did not originate with Tito, yet he was happy to accept it. Among the leading comrades, only Ranković expressed disagreement. But Tito's acceptance of de-Stalinization and de-Leninization did not prevent him, in connection with my revisionism, from regenerating "democratic centralism" and calling me a violator of the decisions of the Sixth Congress.

During a recurrent liberal crisis in 1972, he announced that he did not agree with the decisions of the Sixth Congress! Consistency in practice and practical perseverance were not in Tito's character precisely because he was an authentic politician, a politician cut from the mold of the ideological Leninist Party hierarchy. The slogan "brotherhood and unity" is Tito's, but even that is not original, for the idea of a united royal Yugoslav state was expressed in similar slogans. During the war, in the midst of calamity and bloodshed, that slogan had a practical effect and in that sense it was "Titoistic"—it united us on Yugoslav and Party grounds and nourished the idea of a postwar federal union and the power of the Communist Party.

The idea of the nonaligned movement of governments did not spring from Tito's head; it was foreign in its roots. But Tito swiftly perceived the possibilities that the idea of nonalignment offered Yugoslavia and him personally in the world arena. He became its most energetic spokesman and organizer, wholly in accord with his temperament and his ambitions. That Yugoslavia did not grasp sufficiently early the ineffectuality and deadly division inherent in the movement, that she did not find in time her natural political place in Europe, can be explained only by Yugoslavia's ideological pretenses and the ambitions of her determined leader.

Slogans abounded. "We do not want anything from others —but we will not give up our own either!" "Let us work as if peace will last a hundred years, but prepare as if war will start tomorrow." Although these are now immortalized in marble and bronze, they are not Tito's. They burrowed their way into his mind from popular axiomatic Soviet propaganda or from a synthesis of political positions, and surfaced in moments of rebellion. Tito's speech and style of delivery overflowed with clichés and concepts inherited from Marxism and folk wisdom: "They are driving their pegs into our wheels," "to live according to one's means," "the historical role of the working class," "the worker must receive what is his." And so on. In contrast, in private conversations, which were indeed rare, Tito was lively, spontaneous, folksy.

Tito may not have been able to invent ideas, but he certainly knew how to use them, adapt them, and adjust them. He was able instinctively to extract from this or that ideological assumption exactly as much as was necessary to implement or promote his own goal or policy. When need arose, he would suppress or quietly abandon this or that ideological assumption, only to revive it with renewed emphasis when the situation changed again. The manipulation of ideas, as well as of people and institutions, was one of Tito's political skills.

Even small ideas—small but valuable incentives and projects that emerged from the Central Committee or the government—Tito would claim as his own for use in some future speech or interview. In time, those of us who originated the small but useful ideas accepted this practice as only natural: to the sum of power is awarded the sum of ideas.

6

In the course of my seventeen-year collaboration with Tito, the thought sometimes would cross my mind that for him the Party, Communism, and the people were, in the final analysis, only a means to realize himself and his mandate. I could conceive that he was driven irresistibly in his pursuit, aware only that what he accomplished would be different from and more vital than the social order he had inherited. In that sense, he reminded me of an artist, though he had no interest in art. He solicited the attention of artists, and honored and rewarded them when what they produced reinforced the system and enhanced his own prestige. Philosophy and religion form the spiritual core of politics, but art is still closer to politics by virtue of its creative momentum and its capacity to captivate and charm the politician.

I recall that following my removal from power Tito said to foreign correspondents: "Political death is the most horrible death of all." Does that not confirm Tito's view of the vocation of politics as more important than life itself? Does that not also explain my long memory of that particular remark of Tito's?

After I broke with Tito, I did not substantially change my opinion of him, but I want to expound on that opinion through self-examination, by reflecting on the past and on what I have learned about politics.

Communism, the Party, the working class, the people, workers—in Tito's mind, these were not individual entities; they were indivisible. Of course he said that whatever he did, he did for the people. To a certain extent, he believed this to be true, allowing for contingencies and the task at hand. Thus everything that was done at any given moment was done for Communism.

And the Party—what was Tito's attitude toward it in light of the theoretical datum that the party is the avant-garde, the "most conscious" power in the building of socialism and Communism? Tito knew from Leninist theory that the Party is a means—the principal means, the necessary means—in the struggle for the dictatorship of the proletariat and the creation of a classless society.

Since he interpreted the dictatorship of the proletariat as his own personal power—based on his conviction that power cannot constitute itself or survive except hierarchically—Tito treated the party objectively as a force. But he also treated it subjectively—looking on it as his instrument to accomplish his intentions and fulfill his role.

In the fall of 1953, at the time of the Trieste crisis, I was with him in the White Palace at Dedinje. We discussed my writing, which was beginning to express criticism of Leninist theory and the Leninist remnants in Yugoslavia. Obviously caught in a dilemma, he said: "Well, it's good. You write well. You should write more against the bourgeoisie, which is still influential, particularly psychologically. And you should write for the young people—the young people are the most important. We are not ready yet for democracy; the dictatorship must go on. . . ." The bourgeoisie in most of Yugoslavia was deprived of all opportunity for independent action. It was irrevocably suppressed in the political arena. Thus the idea of writing about the bourgeoisie when Leninist and Stalinist currents and forms were lively and strong would mean wasting my ammunition on a battered, forlorn enemy, shooting in the dark at a faint target. It was clear that Tito had not moved beyond the past, beyond the vanquished time. Perhaps he was unable to do so. But I had already set out on my own path—not altogether aware of what I was doing—the path that would irrevocably take me away from him.

Obviously, Tito knew that the confrontation with the Soviet Union would alter a number of things: the position of the country and its social structure; also, the consciousness of the Communists. This was evident from the speeches he gave at the time, particularly his address to the Sixth Party Congress in 1952. He saw expansion, especially in the realm of ideas, as hazardous and threatening, not only to the system—perhaps less to the system—but also to his position and his historical role. In suppressing "revisionist" democratic ideas and tendencies, he suspected, was even confident, that he would command the support of the dogmatic, power-loving cadres among the political hierarchy. These cadres had knowingly thrown in their lot with him and his autocratic role. At the same time, Tito realized that he could no longer revert to the kind of power he had exercised before the conflict with the Soviet Union, when the Central Committee, in reality as well as in theory, had functioned merely as an arm of his personal apparatus. Regenerated, reconstructed social forms and institutions had to be preserved, and not only as "Titoistic," in view of Tito's *regenerated* new role. If there had been no confrontation with the Soviet

Union, which was sustained by postwar revolutionary pa-
triotism and by self-generated authority, and last but not
least by Tito's determination to preserve his state and his
independent role, the Yugoslav system would have been no
better—and perhaps worse—than the existing systems in
Bulgaria and Romania.

Heeding his wartime practices, Tito exercised power
through people who reported to him personally—the guard,
the secret police, the army—all of whom were independent,
or largely so, of the Party. Only the Party could affirm his
legitimacy: this is the situation in all Communist countries.
Stalin could not rid himself of that legitimacy, not even
after he had executed the majority of the Central Committee in 1934, during the Seventeenth Congress. Tito never
relinquished or neglected that legitimacy, although after
the war he relied on it less than on the army and the police.
Furthermore, after the break with the Soviet Union, he
returned to the Party with restored confidence and zeal.
Never, not even before the struggle with the U.S.S.R., was
Tito's power formally, seemingly totally personal. It was
always—to whatever extent—also the power of the Party.

For Tito, the Party was not just an instrument of revolution and social consolidation. For more than most of the
Communist leaders, the Party offered to Tito an emotional
intellectual stronghold, a purpose in life, a destiny.

In the semiofficial annals in Yugoslavia, everything is presented as "unofficial," but official assent is sought for everything. In the countless publications about Tito and the
Party, Tito is portrayed not only as the man who consolidated the Party, but also as the man who created it. There
is no doubt that Tito's role was the most important, if consolidation is attributed to individuals and not to the wide
circle of revolutionaries and to the broad revolutionary

movement that Tito was nominated to lead in 1937. His role as a "builder" is modest unless we define the role of builder as a member of top leadership. Until the war, he spent the greater part of his time out of the country. As secretary of the Party, he almost never attended the major higher national forums. For instance, he did not participate in a single session of the Regional Committee for Serbia, although he was frequently in Belgrade.

Unquestionably, Tito inspired fortitude and energy in a manner that was fanatical, almost mystical. He merged his personality with the Party, both the tangible Party that had expressed itself in the concrete circumstances of war—which is to say, with living, breathing comrades in arms—and the abstract Party, the Party of ideas. The Communist movement is pragmatic and utopian. Its utopian goal is sustained by science and confirmed by practice. Tito's agile pragmatism was compatible with that goal, demonstrated by the disintegration of the old system, and fostered by revolutionary ferment.

Those deities of the Comintern—international revolutionaries and creators of a new world, Stalin among them, who incarnated the universal wisdom of Marx and Lenin—had bestowed on him the radiant halo of their trust. In Tito, the Communists saw the real thing, their own man, even though his private life and the level of his intellect did not quite correspond to the puritanical standards of the Party literati. One passed over these weaknesses in silence or with idle chatter—concessions to higher goals and the highest, most potent function.

If it were possible to reduce Tito to one single feature, then that feature would be partisanship, the Party. Above all, Tito is the representative and leader of the middle Party ranks. In the prerevolutionary period, that segment was composed of would-be intellectuals, or intellectuals who had abandoned their jobs. It was composed of skilled workers unhappy with their lot, of idealists and dreamers, and a few careerists. With the Party's rise to power, people from all social strata swarmed to join it, people craving political privilege and advancement. The social pattern of that segment has shifted, but not its social function. In the prerevolutionary and revolutionary periods, that segment organized the Party and carried on the struggle; functionaries and leaders emerged from it. And heroes were born of it: Communists are a social and ideological group who will sacrifice, suffer, and even die to advance their goals. After the revolution became a reality, it was mainly from the fighters, the heroes, that the political professionals, the state and Party functionaries, were recruited.

The Party welcomed intellectuals—Tito did, and so did the war combatants—but only if they did not "philosophize," and so long as they sacrificed themselves to the ideals of the working class—in sum, so long as they yielded to the middle segment, and eventually dissolved into it. That middle segment is suspicious of intellectuals, and especially of intellectuals who think and examine, as distinct from specialized scholars. One cannot dispense with intellectuals, and especially with "thinkers" and "literati." But a certain caution toward them is essential.

Tito shared the suspicion and mistrust of intellectuals both within and outside the Party felt by the Party professionals. But he took a broader view, a more flexible approach, certainly broader and more flexible than other Party officials, those Party officials who identified so excessively with the working class—or, more accurately, with the theoretical mission of the working class—that they went beyond self-sacrifice, succumbing to self-abasement and self-abuse.

Often these Party intellectuals would, in official publications, indict their own "petit-bourgeois origins" and their "sense of inferiority." Tito's open and flexible approach to intellectuals may have had its origins in nostalgia for his own inadequate formal education. But even here, his motives were essentially political: without intellectuals, contemporary institutions could not survive, let alone flourish. Who would write propaganda? Who would carry the banners of science and culture and education? Who would build the cities? Who, indeed, would forge the monuments that would glorify the revolution and its leaders? Tito was politically sophisticated. That can hardly be said of the Party professionals.

The middle ranks—those in the Party committees as well as those in the administration—made up the skeleton and nervous system of power. Whenever Tito spoke, and whatever he undertook, he was mindful of those ranks. So were the high Titoist officials. Immediately after the 1949–1950 crisis, the catastrophic results of collectivization, i.e., cooperatives—the Yugoslav version of the Soviet kolkhoz—could no longer be ignored. Actually, what had happened in Yugoslavia did not happen as a result of the displacement of the kulaks and the subsequent wholesale death by famine. There is no Siberia in Yugoslavia, and more prudent and flexible policies were in effect.

In addition, the United States had begun to provide aid in the form of food supplies. But the prisons were overflowing, and the instinctive resistance of the farmers, which had been gathering momentum, pushed us to the brink of self-destruction and national disaster. In 1952, Kardelj and I proposed that the collectives be disbanded. The situation had become absurd. We were receiving aid from the United

States, and on a smaller scale from England and France, although Yugoslavia herself could be self-sufficient. Even today, if a more rational and nonideological policy with respect to agricultural production were to be instituted, we would be able to balance our foreign-trade deficit by exporting food. But Tito did not agree: "We have just begun —we cannot give up socialism in the villages!" His sentiment was endorsed by Party agricultural experts. Even Central Committee member Petar Stambolić said: "It breaks my heart to think of dissolving such enormous collective estates."

So the entire problem was put off for a year, until it reached a level of such chaos and resistance that no one could suppress it. News of a meeting with Kardelj, at which the issue of how to negotiate the abolition of the cooperatives by voluntary departure was to be formulated, had leaked out, and the press was making insinuations about what was in store. Another problem arose: what would happen to a number of disaffected one-time brigadiers and odd-job officials who had found haven and paying political jobs in the cooperatives? The solution was found! Maximum ownership would be reduced from thirty to ten hectares, and the surplus land would be turned into state cooperatives, to which those officials would relocate. The legislation imposing that solution is still in effect today. It has even been courageously proposed that the allotment be increased to twenty hectares in the mountain regions, although Yugoslavia continues to import agricultural products.

Furthermore, Tito's reliance on the middle ranks—a spontaneous, almost organic union—manifested itself in enthusiastic mass receptions, even on such occasions as Tito's trips through the countryside en route to his hunting grounds.

These receptions were not merely the result of organization and pressure. They demonstrated the genuine enthusiasm of local organizations, and that enthusiasm was easily transmitted to the simple-minded and apolitical masses.

It was not like that in those first postwar years. Then the Party leaders, and Tito, too, were closer to the masses. Tito still showed great concern for the well-being of his top people. He even gave his approval for them to occupy villas that had been abandoned and nationalized. He made certain that the restricted shops were well supplied. I remember his order during the winter of 1945–1946 that five tons of coal be allotted to each high federal official. How moved we were! Salaries were low indeed, but we had almost everything we needed free of charge, except for coal, which was so expensive. Relations among us were still idyllic and natural. It never occurred to anyone that it would have been more just to regulate all our supplies, even coal, by legal measures.

But with centralization, with the gradual dwindling of political decision-making, the middle ranks began to lose their revolutionary initiative and transform themselves into a political coalition of the center. Still, politics will find a way to breathe even in an autocracy: in the circle around Tito differences and conflicts began in time to emerge. First, there was the confrontation with the Soviet Union, then democratization (my case), and finally, rival claims of succession (Ranković's case). Tito understood, I believe—more from his conflict with me than from the conflict with the Soviet Union—that the danger to him and his system sprang from the top; only if the top is disunited would such danger filter down to the base foundation, the middle ranks and the people. It cannot be otherwise in a nondemocratic, one-party system. That has been demonstrated most clearly, and most ominously, in the reactions of the mass movement initiated by the nationalist differences of the Croatian Communists.

Tito was irrevocably bound to the Party, and above all to the groups and the ranks, who through ideology and power strive for privilege. At the same time, he did not neglect the rapport he enjoyed with the people. In contrast to most Communist leaders, and particularly Stalin, who fortified his inscrutability and omniscience by retreating into the Kremlin, Tito made frequent appearances at rallies, visited construction sites, enjoyed large audiences. Roars of welcome and applause, streets thick with flowers, and city squares thronged with people captivated him for the moment, while they lasted, perhaps even a little longer than they lasted. He would assess the spectacle rationally, evaluate the mood, and point to the enthusiasm and the splendor of the welcome.

And because he identified the Party with himself, Tito insisted on controlling it. To insure the continuity of that identification, the Party must follow the one who leads it devotedly on its historic course—especially because that guarantees a "happy tomorrow," the transformation of the life of the people. Mistakes are possible, even deviations—particularly in certain government officials. Tito saw in himself a leader, and it was as a leader that he conducted himself, a leader who made his people happy. This charismatic sense of himself was an essential component of Tito's psychology.

That was why he fostered a unique personal relationship with the people, as well as with the army. During the war, when he spent so much time with Partisan units in the villages, he came to know the sorrows and sufferings of the peasant. Defeats shook him, victories delighted him. At

Drvar, in 1944, he was concerned with the future production of nails, because they were essential to reconstruction of houses that had been demolished. In 1946, during a long drought, in the evening he went out of his villa at Dedinje to inspect the sky because weathermen make mistakes, too. With time, with change, as the complexity of the problems deepened, so did Tito's experience of the people and his relationship to them. The problems became the problems not of Yugoslavia alone, but of the whole world. Power and glory dazzled Tito, as they did the Party and the people. Accustomed to privilege, entrenched in power, the Party inevitably elevated Tito above itself. And the people? The people suffered, and coped more or less as they had always done: the link between the leader and the people grew ever more tenuous and abstract, ever more joyful, innocent, bright.

Tito's alliance with the Party—and the middle ranks—remained constant, specific, practical. In that union, in that spark were success, power, and survival. In every crisis, Tito relied on the middle ranks, recognizing in them the most steadfast, most tenacious link in the chain of his power. He had always suspected and known that they were more *personal* than an instrument of the Party and the state. Tito never interfered with, or reproached, the officials who enjoyed luxury and extravagance—except in drastic instances, touching on politics or law. This was not because of his own lack of restraint in comfortable living, but largely because he believed that such license was a natural and hard-won right of an official. The new liberation forces assumed their own mantle of authority; they tailored the law, their own mode of morality, and their customs: so it was, so it must be now, if we are not to put in jeopardy our power, our authority, "everything that we fought for. . . ."

7

There is truth in the observation that for a Communist dictator it does not matter which state he rules. This is also an anti-Communist bias.

What is essential in Communism, regardless of its national base, is power. Power builds a new Communist society. In the actions and aspirations of every authentic Communist leader there is constant drive. A Communist leader, particularly a dictator, is shaped in the long and harsh national struggle.

Taken abstractly, Communist ideology and Communist power are such that it should be a matter of indifference to a Communist autocrat which country he rules. But no ideology is wholly abstract and certainly not wholly pure— one that could be applied in all its aspects to all countries and all situations. As soon as the application begins, this or that conjecture loses or gains weight. So it is with power. Communist leaders, dictators, have distinct personalities. Avtorkhanov astutely observed the futility of building Leonid Brezhnev into a dictator, because of Brezhnev's own inability to transform himself into one.

Fascist and Communist dictators alike are leaders of ideological mass movements. That is not to equate fascism with Communism. The resemblances are only external and formal, because the movements have different social origins and aspirations, different social structures, which they must preserve or build upon. Externally, in their decorative or superficial aspects, Communist dictators resemble fascist dictators. They share the same irresistible drive to personal prominence and personal power. But the manner in which they execute their goals is different. Communist movements and Communist leaders rise from the ruins of old structures and ancient dreams; their power is a process of growth, their forms rejuvenate and change. New forms and new empires emerge from Communism. Communism will leave indelible traces. It will outlast certain Communist states— including the Soviet Union.

Fascism is something intrinsically different. Fascists seek to change political relationships and maintain social conditions. Fascism is nightmare and madness; Communism is force and taboo. Fascism is temporary; Communism is an enduring way of life. Fascist dictators have disappeared or degenerated with the fall of the great fascist powers, Italy and Germany; and contemporary fascist dictators in Latin America, Africa, and elsewhere are merely the chief officers of corrupt coalitions of the military and the police who attempt in vain to build an ideology and a popular movement in order to preserve oligarchic privileges and obsolete forms of government.

In both ideology and intention, a fascist leader is nationalistic. After all, the foundation of Adolf Hitler's Aryan world of the future was to rest on the German nation. Fascist leaders dream of conquests; they plan them, undertake them. The raison d'être of fascism is conquest. A fascist leader seeks to enslave others, but he thinks it natural to rule only his own nation, since he is the complete expression of its will and its fate.

A Communist leader is different: he would agree to rule another country, but that does not mean that he could, or would, know how to. He would argue that he is called by ideological imperatives, by international consciousness; here, totality and perfection are transformed into personal ambitions. But desire and acceptance still do not guarantee the possibility or the capability. Communism that wrests its independence from the Soviet empire instantly sees itself as the most perfect form of ideology while clinging to its nationalistic identity. Communism is international consciousness on national soil. A Communist leader is a national ruler on the international scene.

Unquestionably, the Soviet assault on Yugoslavia in 1948 inflamed Yugoslavia's and Tito's ambitions in the Balkans and toward other national democracies. And it is certainly true that in this period Yugoslavia directed its attention to national realities and possibilities. It was not by chance that Tito then observed with bitter sadness to his closest comrades: "Basically we are not a developed country, and as long as that is the case . . ." However, once Yugoslavia had consolidated its independence, the movement of the non-aligned countries brought both Tito and Yugoslavia into the wider international sphere, and they were to become—now that they had moved beyond Communism—even more of an irritant to the global expansionism of the Soviets.

Tito is something of a foreigner in Yugoslavia. Not so much because he fought on the Austro-Hungarian side in the war that gave birth to Yugoslavia, or because of his seven-year stay in the Soviet Union during a crucial phase of our country's development, or because of his own coming of age at the height of the Soviet Revolution and the purges. He is half foreign by origin and by orientation owing to his Croatian background. The people of Zagorje are emotionally and historically the most Croatian of Croatians. Linguistically and psychologically, Croatia is a world unto itself. It is an island apart in the Yugoslav sea; its language, drawing on a long literary tradition, is a dialect distinguished from the standard idiom of our language. The people are industrious, migratory, lively, fond of good times, wine, and song.

It is irrelevant that some Serbian nationalists see Tito as a successor to the Austro-Hungarians who sought to destroy Serbian power, just as it is irrelevant that Croatian nationalists denounce him as a renegade who hired himself out to the Serbs. What is crucial is that, in spite of his narrow cultural background, he managed to rule the whole of Yugoslavia, a country of manifold nationalities, in which two of those nationalities virtually identify their national essence with statehood. Explanations are available—I have presented some in this book—in the all-Yugoslav, and the only all-Yugoslav, party, the Communist Party, in the preservation of a combined state through revolution, in the consolidation of Yugoslavia as an independent state through its own defense.

But how large was Tito's role in this? Tito's role, like that of every politician, is measured by the scale of his contribution to political and social relationships. In all of this —though I will put some things aside for the moment—what may be most important is how things are solved, rather than what is achieved by the solution. When he took over the leadership of the Party, Tito was immersed in Yugoslav reality, a reality perceived, to be sure, from the Communist point of view and interpreted through the activity of the

Communist Party. The fascist invasion, the war, the capitulation of rival parties, the growth of the power and influence of the Soviet Union, the revolutionary conditions under the occupation—all these confirmed the predictions of the Communist Party. These conditions gave the Party the opportunity to organize and act nationally.

It was necessary to organize continuously, on a day-to-day basis, to shift, to adjust the forms at the right time. In that process, Tito was undoubtedly more enterprising and resourceful than any other Yugoslav revolutionary leader. He had the most spirited and instinctive sense for what was concrete, for what was possible. He was far from infallible—the reality of politics is fluid, elusive—but he quickly recovered his balance and overcame his vagaries, groping for and clutching at the possible and the concrete. He did not acknowledge his errors publicly, certainly not in a direct or repentant manner—not even errors that were obvious and grave. When he caught himself in a mistake, he paused and quietly took note of it. Then, without guilt and without hesitation, he corrected it. In 1951 or 1952, I suggested quite casually that we abolish commissars in the army. Whether by nature or by habit, he defined anything that undermined his prestige or his position, ironically enough, as alien and hostile. He snapped: "Nonsense! What do you want to do, for Christ's sake, destroy the army?" But the position of commissars in the army was abolished several months later. When he made that announcement at a Politburo meeting, he threw a glance at me, without apology, and said: "Well, it is always good to have a few more opinions. . . ."

Tito was never quite able to measure his responsibility for failure; and he was still less able to do so as his personal power grew. He understood only the reality of others, only the mistakes of other people. Consequently, he was given to blaming others easily, sometimes unintentionally, at such times behaving as if he did not have absolute power. He would use such expressions as "I said," "I pointed out," "I was not listened to," "I didn't know," "I was deceived"— expressions that he fell back on to respond to major mistakes or blunders.

In the flood of idolatry and the radiance of his power, I noticed in Tito (especially before my break with him) the gradual decline of his capacity for self-criticism. I believe that his sense of the concrete and the possible was also declining, though not to the same degree as his capacity for self-criticism. Otherwise, Yugoslavia would not have sunk into such economic disaster, would not have plunged into "nonaligned" commitments, would not have experienced a considerable bureaucratic inefficiency. The perfect world, the world without criticism and alternatives, is the world of immeasurable and incurable mistakes.

Yugoslavia and the Communist Party were for Tito immediate but also historical reality. Although Yugoslavia was his own reality, it could not be a world unto himself. He knew this, and sought continuously to step beyond the borders of Yugoslavia, even to impose Yugoslav reality and Yugoslav problems on the world. Firmly and unequivocally, he boasted of Yugoslavia's achievements, her prestige and power, particularly power. "Power" and "powerful" were words he used often.

For a politician, what is concrete and possible is the groundwork and the goal, the means and the justification. But the professional politician like Tito is never content with the specific achievement because he knows that reality is fickle, treacherous, and dangerous. Tito was constantly on the alert, guarding his achievement and his independence.

In the early fifties, when, because of the Soviet blockade, because of the backwardness of our country and our own dogmatism, Yugoslavia was forced to depend on Western aid, chiefly American—and in response to that aid, to make certain adjustments in its foreign policy—Tito expressed his uneasiness and pain to his closest collaborators: "There can be no independence without an independent foreign policy!" He found it particularly galling to accept economic aid. On the other hand, military assistance seemed to him to obligate us less, because Yugoslavia was assertive and ready to defend herself as well as other nations. Therefore, he insisted all the more impatiently after the death of Stalin, in 1953, that Yugoslavia be relieved of the need for Western aid. But since most of the assistance consisted of food—Yugoslavia's agriculture was in disarray—his policy of "doing without" was as senseless as it was impractical.

Yet when the concrete and the possible became the objective of *all* political activity, loss of direction, and ultimately even failure may result. Political theory is essential to political practice; without theory, there is no vision or inspiration in politics. The major flaws in Tito's policies were apparent after the suppression of the democratic currents in the Party and following the reconciliation with the Soviet leadership. Then, he adhered tenaciously, inconsistently, to obsolete Leninist theory and to Kardelj's pragmatic blend of Leninism and social democracy. Because he had no head for theory but an instinct for the necessity of it, Tito embraced Kardelj's theories all the more comfortably—especially since the cooperation with both the East and the West reinforced Yugoslavia's independence and the importance of his own role.

In the fall of 1953, when the United States and Great Britain decided that Zone A—Trieste and its environs—

should be ceded to Italy, Yugolsavia erupted with demonstrations, and Tito threatened to send the army into Zone
A. Though he expressed genuine bitterness, I believe that
his decision was also part of a carefully devised plan to stress
Yugoslav independence from the West at the very moment
when there were indications of changes in the Soviet Union
in the wake of Stalin's death. I went to see him at that time
to get his reaction to my new writings. He was on the telephone with General Kosta Nadj, I believe, giving orders
that our Soviet-built tanks should be sent into the disputed
area, but not our American tanks, which would be embarrassing. I asked him: "How are we going to fire at the
Italians when they are protected by the Americans and the
English? Are we going to fire on them as well?" He answered: "We'll go in if the Italians go in. Then we'll see.
. . ." Shortly thereafter, during a Central Committee meeting at his house, he told us why he felt the measures taken
were inadequate: "If we are not decisive, they will ask for
Zone B, too. That's what I am afraid of."

I maintain that no such danger existed: the United States
and Great Britain wanted simply to get rid of a minor burden, which was poisoning Yugoslav-Italian relations. The
United States and Great Britain soon abandoned their plan,
the hubbub died down, and a year later—in 1954, in London—an agreement was reached by which Zone A was ceded
to Italy and Zone B to Yugoslavia—just as the United States
and Great Britain had originally intended. The emotional
factors in Tito's decision on that matter were important,
perhaps paramount. In politics, these emotional considera-
tions are in fact substantial realities! In another instance,
Tito's concrete and possible were not burdened by the legacy of theory or based on it. "We cannot take Trieste!" he

had told me in 1951, responding to my hesitation during a flare-up in the ongoing Trieste crisis.

In assessing the actions and the personality of a politician, it is their words that mislead most often. And not because politicians are a breed given to concealing their intentions behind a screen of words—that's the nature of the beast. Yet, we recognize that politics, even if infused with high, profound sincerity, is also characterized by concealment, deception, exaggeration, debasement, gossip—every kind of ingenious and unpredictable manipulation of the truth. The reason is that life compressed into politics is inevitably mutable, diverse in its impulses. For a politician to survive, and to succeed, he must determine the right way and the effective means in every situation. For that reason we are on more secure ground if we evaluate politicians on the basis of *how* they speak, rather than on *what* they say. For the manner of speaking reveals the personality—the potentialities and inclinations of the personality—while the content of what a politician says, often unoriginal in itself, masks his personality and distorts his real intentions.

Tito's manner was distinguished by its clarity and simplicity—clarity and simplicity devoid of color and with not a trace of the orator's eloquence. He was clear and simple even when he was attempting to conceal that he was of two minds in certain matters. Everyone understood what he wanted or what he did not want, what he thought ought to be and what ought not to be, particularly those in the middle Party ranks. Those qualities, along with his instinct for what was real, constituted possibly the strongest aspect of his spirit. In fact, the simplicity and clarity of his expression merged with his feeling for the concrete and the possible.

The simplicity and clarity revealed without a doubt that whatever Tito and the Communist Party stood for was real and would materialize, though not without effort and sacrifice. Whenever I hear politicians—particularly those Serbian and Croatian Party leaders who deviated from the Party in 1971–1972—express themselves in an obscure way, I see the unmistakable signs of their decline and fall. That may be because I have myself experienced something similar on two occasions: first, in the summer of 1953 at Brioni, when, on Tito's suggestion, I spoke before the Plenum of the Central Committee, in a show of unity; and again in January of 1954, before the Plenum of the Central Committee, when, denounced and expelled for revisionism, I had acted as a Communist pragmatist: I retracted my ideas, in part because I had bound up their importance and effect exclusively with the Communist Party.

The concrete and the possible, clarity and simplicity— Tito recognized in those qualities means of power, I would even say pure power. On balance, he was less attracted to, or sustained by, the kind of power that subjugates all to itself, that meddles in everything, than he was to the power of the Party, the secret police, and the army. Tito did not make a single decision, not even inadvertently, without assessing it from the vantage point of pure politics, or, rather, of the functioning and advancement of the Party, the secret police, and the army.

Essentially, the same was true in non-Communist political and social systems, however democratic the structure of state bureaucracy and the decision-making process. Quite simply, what distinguishes systems from one another is the strength of the right to choose and the right to criticize political leadership. That life in Yugoslavia, in contrast to the rest of the Communist states, is better, more tolerable, is the result of many elements, one of which—absurd as it may seem —is Tito's pure politics, and Tito's more autocratic than totalitarian rule. Precisely because of the secondary importance he assigned to other areas—to the economy, to culture, to sport, and so on—in relation to the primacy of pure power, pure politics, these other areas resisted dogmatism and oppression and developed partial independence. Tito's appetite for luxury—another absurdity generated by politics —provoked in others a desire for consumption, which loosened up social and cultural differentiations.

If Yugoslavia was too small for Tito, Tito was too big for Yugoslavia. But let us put aside theory and conclude with St. Augustine: A sinner is better than an automaton.

8

No political system is shaped wholly by the will of its leaders. Not even during the most intense terror and the most rapid collectivization did the Soviet system reflect fully the programs and methods of Stalin. A social system rises from the interplay of spontaneous energies generated at the bottom and organizational structures at the top. Political skill is to initiate the interplay between the spontaneous and the structured.

In the example of the postwar Yugoslav system, we find the Party masses swarming toward the acquisition of all kinds of privilege. We find the spontaneous resistance of the "nonsocialist" segments to the new system. We find an organized oppression of all areas of life. In this respect, Yugoslavia, having passed through the crucible of revolution, differed from the other national democracies only to the degree that its oppression was more radical and comprehensive. Although considerable areas of private possession were spared—farm property, private houses, small companies—lawlessness and coercion accelerated to the point that internally Yugoslavia bore a stronger resemblance—similarity, not identity—to the Soviet Union than to any other national democracy. But the West was wrong when it labeled Yugoslavia the "Number-one satellite," because we Yugoslavs agreed with Moscow more than we listened to Moscow. What's more, we argued with Moscow secretly, and even vied over the avant-garde role in the development of Communism. Where the Soviet Union can be validly compared with Yugoslavia is in pure politics, in pure power, which was the stronghold of Josip Broz Tito.

The bureaucracy proliferated incessantly. Only when one held a bureaucratic post was one offered stability and perspective. Not even the agencies of oppression—particularly of political oppression, the secret police—were an exception, in spite of the stringent conditions under which they were hired. At the beginning, such agencies had been staffed by steadfast Party members, devoted, unwavering Communists. But political careerists and postrevolutionary revolutionaries gradually were attracted to these positions. The effects of the control that the secret police exerted over all areas of life—seeping into all the pores, infiltrating family and private life—were poisonous for society as well as for the ruling Party. In 1947 my first wife, Mitra, confided in me that even the members of the Central Committee for Serbia were careful about what they said in the presence of the comrade in charge of the secret police. If that was the situation in Belgrade, what must it have been like in the provincial committees?

The concept of Party control through the secret police—one group of Communists monitoring another—was unquestionably the invention of Moscow, of Lenin and of Stalin. Tito and the "Titovites" merely took it from there. But we would have come up with that invention in any case, most probably when the Party expanded after the end of the war. To control expansion and to prevent the Party from falling prey to counterrevolutionary forces and foreign influences, the secret police becomes an instrument of power at the top, the master above new masters. A major consequence is that the role of the Party diminishes and, with it, the activity and the initiative of the lower ranks of the Party.

After the break with Moscow, a number of things changed, generally for the better, but the power and omnipresence of the secret police grew. In the beginning, because of pro-Soviet activities, the role of the secret police was inevitable and understandable. Yet that role did not change after the slackening of tension with the U.S.S.R. and after the death of Stalin. It did not diminish even after the authority of law was reinstated in nonpolitical areas. Change *did* come—though it was superficial and short-lived—in 1966, when the revolutionary police system had begun to outlive its usefulness, when Tito suspected or discovered a plot in the ranks of the secret police. By all accounts, the plot was not directed against Tito himself, but it could have led to a weakening of his power. The majority of officers in the secret police were retired or transferred to other services. And, at least in theory, the secret police was then treated as a specialized service.

Democratic trends soon began to make themselves felt within the Party—nationalistic in Croatia, liberal in Serbia, technocratic in Slovenia. Tito adjusted to these trends and changes, but remained himself immutable in the preservation of his personal power. This most liberal period of Tito's rule was marked by diminished personal and doctrinal aggression.

Within five years, however, these non-Leninist trends had gathered such momentum that they posed a threat to the

"Titoist" system and, by extension, to Tito himself. In 1971–1972, with the aid of the army, Tito purged the Party and returned the secret police to his direct control.

He was formally accorded absolute power—the presidency of both the Party and the state "for life." He rarely attended the meetings of the Presidium; deputies came to him to report. A program of indoctrination was initiated, and Yugoslavs of all ages, from children to the very old, were exposed to "Tito's style of Marxism." In his own country, he was the only acknowledged adulated presence. In the world, in the Communist and capitalist countries and in the nonaligned countries, he was hailed as a statesman without peer.

So it was that the system, the social order, underwent substantial change, while Tito's role and mode of exercising power remained essentially intact. That would not have been possible if power had not been the cornerstone of the system, if the Party were not the basic unit of society; power and Party, even detached to a large degree from ideology, still retain institutionalized authority. To be precise: Tito himself changed, his rule changed, and he was the one to effect the change. This absurdity of politics confounds even the dialectics: Tito was able to remain immutable, to continue to fortify his pure power, because he did not inhibit change in other areas of the system, perhaps not in the system as a whole. It is not accidental that in the nonpolitical areas—for instance, in the economy and culture—Tito very seldom took an initiative. But it is equally true that when a certain reform or shift in policy won acceptance—and especially when it proved fruitful—Tito endorsed it with wholehearted enthusiasm. When Kidrič and other Party economists and theoreticians sought to gear the economy to an open market, Tito could not have reacted with more energetic support. His support took the form of a clear and simple measure: changing the value of the dinar. But this did not relate economics to other aspects of policy.

Until the very end Tito did not accept the view that political activities—the salaries of Party officials, youth-group projects, revolutionary celebrations—could be measured in dinars. He held that politics has standards that cannot always be measured by the laws of economics.

If, after the 1948 confrontation with the Soviet Union, Yugoslavia had continued as an administrative system based on the Soviet economic model, she would have fallen into chaos, which might have undermined the power of the state and Tito's power, however indivisible they were. That would have given rise to the possibility of foreign intervention—primarily Soviet military intervention—which would have inhibited national development for decades. In order to function effectively, economic enterprises and management were given autonomy, but only insofar as it did not infringe on Party authority. The same was true of culture, so long as it did not deal with subjects that were taboo, meaning the Party, the revolution, and of course Tito himself. Everything began to take on a nonideological market value.

Anti-Stalinism and the free market became incompatible because of bureaucratic values and the omnipotence of the police. Yet the concept of self-management was born from the struggle against Stalinist tyranny and from visions of a true democratic socialism. Self-management legalized criticism of the bureaucracy. It also suppressed bureaucratic willfulness. And it solidified gains toward a free-market economy. But it did not substantially influence the character of power, or of political circumstance. In the context of a monolithic Party, an omnipresent secret police, and an autocratic leader, self-management could not effectively become democratic. All political crises in Yugoslavia took place outside of self-management: the power of the secret police waxed and waned; currents of opposition were spawned in the Party independently; and not a single strike, literally not one—though in recent years there were numerous economic skirmishes—was initiated by the organs of self-management or by the unions.

Briefly: self-management is undoubtedly an achievement in the area of the rights of producers and of a free-market economy, but it has no influence on power and the political system—on pure politics. Moreover, in the course of the last ten years—following the purges in Croatia and Serbia, the comprehensive program of indoctrination, and Tito's elevation to absolute rule for life—the focus of Party activity has been concentrated on the self-governing agencies, which increased their Party membership to over ninety percent. Thus, self-management ought to have provided the most important sector of Party activity. The most prominent theoretician of "democratic totalitarianization" was Kardelj, notably in his last work, *Trends of Development in the Political System of Socialistic Self-Management,* which, incidentally, won considerable admiration among certain socialists in the West.

Precisely because self-management evolved from creative opposition to Stalin and the Soviet system, and precisely because it failed to limit the political bureaucracy of the Party, it provided the basis for a new kind of ideological mobilization. Self-management assumed utopian inspiration, which is to say, socialist "theory."

Tito was never exactly passionate about self-management. Nor could he be, unless he was willing to subject his own power to critical evaluation. But that was not the issue. Tito supported self-management. In 1950 he even formulated the law that set it in motion. He understood that to make self-management absolute, to invest it with ideology, would strengthen national independence and underline the singularity of Yugoslavia. But he would not go beyond that: self-management could not overstep, let alone put in jeopardy, the system of government conceived in the revolution, the system that corresponded to his own aspirations and beliefs. The real fused with the ideal: an incomplete market economy resulted. How could it be otherwise with the forms of ownership which favored the monopoly of a political power? An idealized reality rarely disturbed Tito's true reality.

The market economy facilitated the process of production and opportunities for employment. Yugoslavia opened its borders to tourists. Law and order were binding now even for those who administered them. The persecution of political opponents changed: penalties were alleviated and standardized, although even today political enemies may be, and often are, sentenced to prison for many years simply for recounting anecdotes or expressing "hostile" opinions among a group of friends. This mechanism of surveillance and the subjection of citizens to political scrutiny remains intact.

I will cite several examples, from memory, and for the purpose of illustration, that will reveal changes in the treatment of political opponents, in continued surveillance, and in power exerted by the political bureaucracy over its citizens.

I recall that in 1945 Cyrus Sulzberger in the *New York Times* speculated that there were fifty thousand anti-Communist guerrillas active in Yugoslavia. The Yugoslav leadership—and I count myself part of it, particularly because I was in charge of propaganda—denounced Sulzberger's figures as malicious misinformation. In fact, his assessment may have been closer to the truth than our own at the time. We had counted forty thousand renegades from the defeated counterrevolutionary armies. There were murderers and gang leaders among them, but also a good number who, by the current revolutionary, doctrinal, and emotional criteria, did not deserve to be imprisoned, let alone executed. A substantial number, perhaps the majority, of the renegades surrendered. But a considerable number stayed in the forests. True, a few committed major crimes, such as murdering Party and state officials, or robbing stores and collectives. They would hardly have been that few if the Party and the authorities had not been so determined and ingenious in tracking them down, whipping up popular opinion against them, and putting pressure on their accomplices. Those who were captured in a skirmish or flushed out of their hiding places were automatically killed, without any legal procedures—most often, on the spot. Usually, they were bitter opponents of the new regime. But among them, as always and everywhere in ideological struggles, there were also men not given to crime. Nonetheless, all were treated the same way. How many of them there were, no one can say for sure. There were no criteria for assessing guilt. By wartime revolutionary criteria they were all guilty: those who aided their leaders, lifted the morale of those around them, built shelters, or frightened the population. And in Yugoslavia, where revolution coincided with the struggle against the occupation forces, counterrevolutionaries and collaborators were considered traitors. The breadth of the revolutionary program did not mitigate the fury of the battle.

In my book *Wartime,* I stated that late in 1945 Tito stopped these perfunctory executions, being carried out by the secret police (OZNA). "Nobody is afraid of capital punishment any longer!" Tito cried out at a Politburo meeting, excited and aware of what the terrible reality had become. Not long thereafter capital punishment was virtually eliminated, and today Yugoslavia has one of the lowest rates of capital punishment in the world, in large part owing to Tito's attitude.

But court proceedings were not accorded to these outlaws except in special cases. Whether this was due to ideological rigidity, raging hatred, or a fierce desire to settle accounts, who can say? In these circumstances, vagaries operated: the mood of the prosecutors, local relationships, private vendettas. However, I firmly believe that the basic issue was the revolutionary, which is to say nonjudicial, character of absolute authority. Tito believed in legal procedures, but not of the kind that restrict the political decision-making process or challenge the primacy of the state. "The church cannot be above the state!" he emphasized in 1945, when he was discussing the dispute over Archbishop Stepinac with a group of comrades.

I often had the opportunity, while touring the country, to listen to security officials who had tracked down and wiped out renegades. They all boasted of their own cleverness or that of their comrades. But they would gloss over failed plans and executions. In the company of his closest friends, Ranković described in minute and colorful detail the most important and dramatic raids. I was already convinced that in settling accounts with the renegades, the governing principle was the primacy and the functioning of the new regime. To be fair, I must add that this principle was not exclusively Communist, or, for that matter, exclusively Yugoslav. Such was the fate that always lay in wait for renegades and rebels in the Balkans. And elsewhere, too, though less frequently in the rest of Europe. I dealt with this subject, in fictional form, in my novella *Intersection*. Writers in Yugoslavia have never touched on the theme of the renegades—not only because the subject might be taboo, but also because they have little knowledge of it and no idea of its interest and significance.

That principle was demonstrated in the following two rather major instances, though neither of them posed a threat to the social system or to the government. In the winter of 1948–1949, a rebellion of Moslem peasants broke out. Five or six hundred peasants gathered together from different villages and set off on the road leading to Cazin, in Bosnia. Along the way, they seized a police station and disarmed a government official from Croatia who happened to be driving by. The commander in charge of a nearby garrison refused to intervene, because he had no orders from above, an action that later led to his dismissal. But some ten to twenty security officers and committee members snatched up their weapons—they also had an automatic machine gun —and set up a position on top of a hill overlooking the town. When the peasants, yelling and shouting, came within range, they opened fire in warning, and the mob dispersed. As a result, no one was wounded. Most of the rebels went back to their villages, as if nothing had happened. But thirty or so who were guilty, or felt guilty about it, fled into the forest: a few days later, all were caught and shot to death on the spot.

Belgrade watched carefully. Two weeks later, when a report was put together, giving a full account of the incident, Kardelj drew my attention to the special quality of the event. "A typical mess," he remarked. "All of it deriving from peasant stories and fancy. Totally disorganized—no clear goal." And indeed, so it was!

We had been afraid of a pro-Stalin disturbance; instead, we had a peasant counterrevolutionary uprising. The Cazin Moslems are a world unto themselves: a warlike and fanatic people, living for centuries in a pocket between Austria and Turkey. During the Partisan war, after a period of vacillation, they finally allied themselves with the Partisans, although as a separate army. Obviously they had been alienated by forced collectivization, but they had no more reason to complain than anyone else. Yet, what was most curious and most unexpected was what incited them to rebel. Nothing in their religious or ethnic background disposed them toward the Serbian monarchy. Yet the rumor that King Peter II had been dropped by parachute somewhere in their region set them off.

It was at the beginning of winter at that same time, 1948–1949, that eleven or twelve pro-Soviet regional and town officials in Bijelo Polje, led by the Secretary of the Regional Committee, Ilija Bulatović, fled into the forest. Not only did they get no support from anyone, but also the people of their region, to the last man, joined the forces which were tracking them down. Defeated, disbanded, the renegades turned themselves in, one after another, without resistance. Yet not a single one made it back into town alive. All were killed en route.

Curious, indeed, is peasant psychology: when the official security guards demonstrated to the peasants how to form a chain across the mountains to prevent the renegades from slipping over the border into Albania, the peasants told these former Partisans openly, "We learned that from the Chetniks when they mobilized us against the Partisans in 1943."

I had known Ilija Bulatović well before the war. He was an honest man, modest, somewhat given to philosophizing, like other peasants who had had a year or two of high school, but he had picked up Marxism in Party schools. On June 28, 1948, after the publication of the Cominform Resolution against Yugoslavia, Bulatović had sent me a letter, as an old acquaintance, and warned the Central Committee not to betray the Soviet Union and drown the country in the waters of imperialism! When he came to Belgrade in July, as a delegate to the Fifth Party Congress, I invited him to lunch to discuss the matter. He told me haltingly and dejectedly that he now agreed with the Central Committee, and blamed his letter on personal distress. I recall hoping that Bulatović, like so many officials more important than he, would resolve the dogmatic and moral dilemmas caused by doubts at that time.

The case of Bulatović and his comrades is perhaps the most dramatic example of the treatment of the pro-Soviet Communists, but not the most typical. Except for those who escaped to other East European countries, all not killed were sent to a camp to serve out their sentences. In Yugoslavia there was, strictly speaking, only one camp, on the island of Goli Otok, on the Dalmatian coast.

That is a taboo subject. No one has written anything about it except Antonije Isaković. His novel dealing with Goli Otok was denied publication two years ago, but recently I heard that it might be published. The subject is truly important in every respect. I cannot avoid it here, not only because of Tito's involvement, but also because of my own: Goli Otok has haunted me both intellectually and morally since my own break with the system, and my reevaluation of it.

It was in the fall of 1948 that Tito made the decision to house the Cominformists at Goli Otok—without consulting the Central Committee, the Politburo, or the secretaries of

the Central Committee, which is to say, Kardelj and Ranković and me. I heard of the decision while I was in Montenegro. Andro Mugoša, a member of the Montenegrin Central Committee, told me that an order had been received
from Belgrade for the arrest of the Cominformists. They
were to be shipped off to the camp at Goli Otok. Ranković
must have known of the decision early, simply because his
bureaucratic apparatus was needed and responsible for the
implementation of the order. Presumably, the decision was
made in great haste. When the arrests began, the camp was
not ready—if indeed there had been any preparations at all.

I can only speculate as to why Tito skipped over the Central Committee and his closest long-time comrades. In the
Central Committee he would not have met with any substantial opposition, yet perhaps he suspected a strong resistance (or hesitation) at the top. It was common knowledge that there were federal ministers, deputies, members
of the republican Central Committees, favorably disposed
toward the Soviet Union and the Cominform. By nature,
Tito was not morbidly suspicious, but he was vigilant and
cautious. Although the atmosphere was tense and poisoned
by conspiratorial moods, we were continuously surprised to
learn that this or that high official was wavering, that he was
expressing support for the Cominform. Stalinists were soon
discovered in every institution of national life. Slanderous
and threatening pro-Soviet propaganda addled the brains
of many. Suspicion wormed its way into the souls of all who
felt responsible for the state and the Party.

At the onset of the troubles, Ranković said with great
distress: "The worst thing is that you don't know who your
enemy is! Yesterday's friend becomes today's enemy—the
enemy in one's own house!" If Tito was more suspicious

than the others, it was because of his experience in the Soviet Union. There was, too, the weight of his responsibility. In 1951, Tito asked Ranković what was the matter with me, because I seemed anxious and depressed. Ranković told him that I had fallen in love with a comrade from the Central Committee, who was to become my second wife, Štefanija. Tito shrugged: "Oh, that. I thought it was something serious."

Perhaps Tito was led to make his sudden, solitary decision—this seems to me the most persuasive explanation—by reports about the rising tide of Stalinists in the Party committees and among the army officers. Although the most outspoken and most militant Stalinists had been arrested, the Cominformists appeared to be multiplying. The arrests of Sreten Žujović and Andrija Hebrang were not discussed in the Central Committee either. Tito made that decision on his own. I suppose it can be argued that it was an incomplete Central Committee. It was elected in 1940 at the Fifth Party Congress but its Plenum did not meet until March 1948, and then to answer the letter of Molotov and Stalin that criticized the Yugoslavs for deviation.

In the notes to his official *Collected Works*, Tito maintains that the Central Committee could not have met because of the circumstances of war. This is nonsense. The time was three years after the war! There had indeed been plenty of time for leisure and hunting. Couldn't the Central Committee have met during the war, just as the Partisan assembly know as AVNOJ had met? The truth is that the Central Committee met when Tito needed its legal support. He needed its support against Stalin and wanted a full forum. Prior to that, the Politburo had met irregularly, with coopted members. The attack by Stalin accelerated the convocation of the Fifth Party Congress and the reorganization at the top. It impelled Tito to initiate a degree of tolerance and to seek cooperation in a collective action.

Spontaneously, to be sure, but not without careful consideration of a tide of facts, Tito translated his sense of danger into knowledge and, further, into a form of defense. The horrors were spawning, mounting. The way out was almost ready-made—the way out came from the Soviet Union. Nor was Tito the only one to see it! My thoughts were drifting in that direction, too, although the news about the camp, and other drastic measures, I accepted with discomfort. Sometime before the Cominform Resolution of June 28, 1948, I said to Ranković casually, as our car was making a turn at Dedinje, "Now we are treating Stalin's followers as he treated his enemies." Almost in despair, Ranković retorted: "Don't say that! Don't talk about it!"

In retrospect, and with all the self-criticism of which I am capable, I must admit that we could not have avoided a concentration camp for the Cominformists. Our Party was in its literal sense Stalinist and it had a monopoly of power. Had it shown tolerance; had it allowed the legalization of opposition within the Party; had it compromised its defense against the aggressive pressure of the Soviet Union and the Communist Parties within the Eastern European bloc—had the Party allowed these, they might have led to the disintegration of the Party and to the ascendancy of pro-Soviet forces. It is the misfortune of dictatorial and particularly totalitarian powers that they cannot allow opposition without undermining their own survival. Besides, the pro-Soviet forces were more Stalinist than our own leadership. The ascent to power of those forces—and there could have been no doubt in anyone's mind about that—would have meant not only the removal of our present leadership

and bloody purges within the Party, but also the subjuga-
tion of Yugoslavia to the Soviet Union.

We are a synthesis of our revolutionary power, of Leninist dogma and Stalin's teaching. Power prevailed; power
was our reality. Still, there was Goli Otok. Although we
did not treat the Cominformists with Stalinist barbarism,
we did not know how to avoid the concentration camp.

The arrests were already under way when a hastily drawn
up law regarding the camp was pushed through the National Assembly. The wording was clumsy and naïve. But it
was functional in the use of a term, "socially beneficial
work," for which the security chiefs had a certain taste.
Prison sentences meted out by the security forces usually
amounted to two years, but the terms could be extended in
the camp.

Evil and shame—evil beyond compare, unending shame—
is what lay in store for the prisoners in the camp. Never
mind the foul food, the mindless and exhausting labor in
the quarry, the prisoners were subjected to torture, the
cruelty of which was matched by its perversity. The security
officers were given the task of reeducating the prisoners and
were instructed to avoid using force. Tito even, in his
speeches, boasted that we were reeducating the prisoners.
The secret police recruited teams from the ranks of the
penitent and organized them into "self-managing units"—
that is exactly what they were called. These units then took
over the task of reeducation, through violence.

The duality of Yugoslav Communism in that period—not
to be as inhuman as Stalinism, but to achieve results not too
dissimilar—was revealed by the camp. It was revealed in the
most monstrous way. On boarding the boat to Goli Otok,
prisoners were shoved head first into its hold, and, on land-
ing, they were herded through a double row of security

guards, who punched and kicked them. This practice, which is referred to in Isaković's novel as the "principle of the frightened rabbit," was frequently tested on the so-called incorrigibles. There were lynchings, too. Those who would not repent were subjected to humiliating abuse, which could only result from the dogmatic fury and the ingenuity of those who had reformed. Prisoners had their heads plunged into pails of human excrement. They were forced to wear placards that read "Traitor." They were required to confess publicly their nonpolitical sins. All of this was carefully planned.

It is not as if no one in Belgrade knew what was going on at Goli Otok. People had their suspicions. I, too, began to suspect from the public retractions of certain persons and from random bits of information. But not even Ranković, the head of the secret police, knew the worst. He returned from a visit to Goli Otok—it must have been in the summer of 1952—moved and delighted by the welcome he had received from the inmates, which is to say, the comrades who had seen the error of their ways. We must change our attitude toward them, he maintained. In September of 1953, I spent some time at the resort of Niška Banja with the writers Dobrica Ćosić and Oskar Davičo. We talked about the new, liberal trends that resistance to Stalin and the Soviet bloc had unleashed in our Communism. I heard that Ćosić, out of curiosity, had visited Goli Otok. He told me that the security service, the UDBA, had devised and applied corrective methods that were possibly the most diabolical in history. When I returned to Belgrade, I told Ranković what I had heard from Ćosić and arranged for Ćosić to report it directly to Ranković. Kardelj also attended the meeting. He shouted in anger: "I knew something vile was going on there!" Ranković ordered an investigation. The situation soon underwent improvement, but the camp was not closed.

Approximately fifteen thousand Party members and sympathizers passed through the camp. A substantial number served time simply because of having expressed pro-Soviet sentiments among friends. Some were entirely innocent. There were also quite a few activists who spread propaganda and tried to organize the overthrow of the regime. The inmates were not provided with the protection of the law; nor were they allowed visits from their families. The camp was, in fact, a source of information for further arrests: to betray an ally still at large was the best way to demonstrate one's own rehabilitation and repentance.

If we take into consideration the fact that among army officers there was a substantial number of Cominformists, seven thousand, I believe, the possible danger to the system was not negligible. But viligance was carried too far. Very few, if any, returned from Goli Otok unscathed. Not so much physically, perhaps, as psychologically and intellectually. Many were bitter, depressed, shattered. Even wise and well-intended ideological reeducation—let alone the forced methods of Goli Otok—leads inevitably to aberration and tragedy if it goes on without public control. Public control is the only control.

Although I was not involved directly in the organization and management of the camp, my ideological activity was not to be ignored. The sharpness and depth of my criticism of Stalin and the Soviet system contributed to the sufferings of the inmates. My positions were taken as official and prescribed. Those who were believed to harbor doubt were forced into self-criticism—in what ways, and with what results, one can only imagine. But doubt arose in me, too. At the end of 1949, when I returned from the United Nations session in New York, I had already begun to think heretical thoughts.

While at the United Nations I observed that the official West viewed the persecution of the Cominformists with understanding, but not without malice. Of course there were humanitarian protests as well. At the meeting during which I reported to Tito on the activity of our delegation to the United Nations, I urged that some thought be given to dissolving the camp, that those who were guilty should be, instead, handed over to the courts. Kardelj was the first to oppose my recommendations. "We need the camp now desperately!" If I remember correctly, Ranković remarked that it would not be so easy to settle accounts with the Cominformists through normal procedures. Tito was silent, reflective, then he dismissed my proposal, probably on the ground that it was premature. And so we reacted in the typical fashion of politicians who are above public control—in pursuit of political goals, arbitrarily and without overriding concern for human conditions, human suffering.

At the plenary meeting of the Central Committee on April 12, 1948, which was the first such meeting since the election of the Central Committee in 1940, and the one at which the reply to the condemnation from Molotov and Stalin was drafted, Tito shouted out: "Our revolution is honest! Our revolution does not eat its children!" This statement, however encouraging to himself and others, was not true at that time. Through its resistance, the Yugoslav revolution was beginning to repay a debt to its Leninist and Stalinist components—to eat its children who continued to be faithful to old faiths. The arrests and the camp for Cominformists confirm this unbearable cruelty. Yes, that's the way it is: the revolution that does not eat its children is not a real revolution, just as the children who because of their revolutionary illusions allow the revolution to devour them are not real revolutionaries.

In the state that Josip Broz Tito created and which created him, the absence of public notice, of public information and discussion, at least within the ruling Party, led to the crisis with the Cominformists. It led to all kinds of excesses and aberrations. The ban on freedom of information is the source of evil in Communist regimes, and in Tito's and Yugoslavia's. This evil permeates society, seeps into its pores, prevents organic development, impels dictatorial authority to terror and violence.

If only there had been freedom of information, if only it had been possible to debate openly . . . But that would have been a different Yugoslavia, a third Yugoslavia, of which, for the time being, we can only dream. There would have been no camp at Goli Otok. Even if there had been a camp, if the will of the leader and the intractable secret police had not dominated the Party, the regime in that camp would not have been such a monstrous combination of two right-minded groups, the security officials and the reeducated.

If only, if only . . . If only we had done things differently, so many problems would have been avoided. For example, deep down, Kardelj was opposed to collectivization, although he had delivered a report in favor of the collectives at the Central Committee Plenum in 1949. For many years there would have been no forced selling. Kidrič, the chief economist, finally called forced selling a form of robbery. Yet that was not its most sinister aspect. I remember Kidrič announcing at a Politburo meeting that sixty-five thousand freight cars of wheat had to be bought on a forced basis. While Ranković was noting down the figure, he groaned: "Twelve thousand arrested!" These peasants were released after two or three months, but what an atmosphere those arrests and the accompanying brutality created! What despair and misery!

Today, undeniably, it is no longer quite like that. The system has evolved and changed in every respect, except that the mechanism of government, the monopoly on information, and the decision-making process are such that, if need be, the entire cycle could be repeated.

Now they arrest selectively. I am not talking about terrorists and spies, who must be arrested, and are arrested everywhere. I am talking about those who are considered too independent or rebellious, or those who have made statements to friends or "official friends" or have met with émigrés. Almost always one can find "enemy propaganda," because "enemy propaganda" can mean anything from complaints about commodity prices to ordinary comments on the scarcity of housing. Actually, they no longer arrest people for such reasons—but, God forbid, should the need arise to do so, they would do so. Three or four such selective arrests can intimidate a town, if not a whole region.

Sometimes Tito refuted charges by foreign countries that there was no freedom in Yugoslavia and that he himself was opposed to freedom. He did so in 1978 at the Belgrade conference on the Helsinki Accords, and during the human-rights campaign in Yugoslavia. No one thinks his justice is not universal. As Marx observed, no one is opposed to freedom in general, only to that freedom which jeopardizes his own power. Tito was for such selective freedom, as Kardelj was for "freedom by degrees," for freedom "in proportion to the rise of consciousness." If that were not so, Tito would not have been faithful to himself, to his Communism and his power.

For Tito was faithful to pure power. That power enabled

him to put his stamp on every aspect of social and national life, a stamp that will show despite new leaders, even if they try to dissociate themselves from Tito's "willfulness," "capriciousness," and "low standards."

Sometimes an opportunity arises for a man to transcend himself, his potential. But no one can transcend his accomplishments. Under Tito, life continued to struggle, to push forward, to send out new shoots. Tito did not want to suppress his power, let alone transcend it.

9

Even during the war, Josip Broz Tito demonstrated his predilection for palaces. At that time, he showed an even greater predilection for caves. The mountains of Bosnia and Montenegro do not teem with palaces, only with caves, which provided a suitable shelter from air raids. For Tito, luxury was separated from life only in times of great calamity and only when his life's work, or his life itself, was at stake.

When we seized control of a town, Tito would choose the finest building for himself, or it would be chosen for him. We had an ideal place at Užice in 1941, the impressive National Bank, which also had the advantage of an underground tunnel to serve as a shelter. It was risky to linger in open spaces. Tito sought caves and forests, or the underground shelters the royal government had built just before the war but never had the opportunity to use. Other wartime leaders shared Tito's predilection for palaces. But Tito's propensity was the most striking, the most organic. I think it sprang from the same source as his desire for absolute power and autocratic rule.

A few days after the liberation of Belgrade, on October 20, 1944, by Yugoslav and Soviet forces, Tito made a tour of inspection of the royal palaces at Dedinje and ordered their restoration. Actually, the palaces had suffered more from neglect than from the direct effects of war. The furniture and china were untouched. Prince Paul's White Palace was in worse shape than King Alexander's palace, known as the Old Palace. Both palaces are located in a wooded area on a hill, commanding good views. But they are not overwhelming. Compared to European counterparts, they seem more like villas, spacious and opulent villas. Tito's preference was for Prince Paul's White Palace. It was brighter and more modern, though designed in the neoclassical tradition. King Alexander's Old Palace was built in the so-called Serbian, Byzantine or Balkan, style.

Before the war was over, the White Palace was repaired and Tito moved in. Tito also retained the Royal Palace and the villa on Romanian Street (renamed Užička Street after 1948). The Royal Palace was set aside for official guests. It was in this palace that the Central Committee met on April 12–13, 1948, to draft a reply to the Soviet letter attacking Yugoslavia. This was also the setting for the Central Committee meeting of June 29, 1948, at which the rebuttal to the Cominform Resolution was drawn up. It was not chance that determined Tito's choice of the Royal Palace for these meetings: no major meetings had been held there, so the odds were high that the rooms were not bugged, and the odds were against the palace being raided or sabotaged.

In those first few years after the war, Tito spent the greater part of his working day in the White Palace, and lived in the villa on Romanian Street. That villa, with its spacious garden, had been the property of a well-to-do Serb by the name of Acević. During the war, the Germans req-

uisitioned it for the use of Minister of Economics Neu-
hausen. After the war, the Communists confiscated it. It is
probably the most beautiful and most comfortable villa in
Dedinje. While the battle of Belgrade was still raging at the
war's end, the First Army set it aside for Tito. Later, Tito
annexed several neighboring villas and their gardens, and
had a stone wall built to enclose the complex. He developed
a special feeling for that villa. He not only lived and worked
in it, but also received visitors there, except on formal occasions.

By protocol and law, Tito had no right to the royal palaces. He was not the chief of state. The President of the
Presidium, Dr. Ivan Ribar, went along with other members
of the Presidium and voiced no objections. All were satisfied
with what had been assigned to them. Not even during the
period of the royal regency, after the coalition government
was formed with representatives of the royal government,
did anyone object. Not even the royal regents objected, or
the royal ministers. True, the King, under pressure from
the British, had to accept the regents we Communists designated. The same was true of royal ministers. But the
regents were content with their prestigious, however transi-
tional, role; and they cared little about the property of the
crown, a crown they represented only formally. Victors take
everything except the spirit, which they cannot shackle.

Nor did other members of the Central Committee criticize Tito. As fellow revolutionaries, they certainly had the
right to do so, but they were content with their success,
with their duties and prospects under Tito's leadership.
Apart from minor personal differences, all were for the
same power, all were for Tito. Doubt and criticism, if they
existed at all, were suppressed lest they be interpreted as
factionalism or morbid ambition. All had become the will-

ing slaves of Party and ideological unity. All would be alienated and helpless outside their milieu, their own utopia.

Tito's predilection for luxury was inseparable from, though incidental to, his willful appropriation of palaces. In this, as in everything else, what was essential for Tito was twofold power, absolute power over the state and over the Party. In the eyes of the people, palaces are the seats and symbols of power. The common people may not be happy that funds are squandered on palaces or on extravagances of their ruler, but they see it as natural and inevitable: wealth may not always be accompanied by splendor, but power always is, or at least it gives the appearance of being so. After the revolution, the theory of the divine origin of power was no longer plausible. Yet the people continued to defer to power as to something uncommon, sublime. Does not power influence human and national destiny?

Thus, while common people may not have thought it right for Communist officials to install themselves in palaces and villas, they did not object loudly. It has always been so in uprisings and wars. Some people did sneer at the promises, at the word that life would be different when the Communists came to power, a time of self-denial, moderation, and equality. But, generally, people saw nothing unusual in Tito's moving into the royal palaces. He was the leader. Power was in his hands. It followed.

Josip Broz Tito sensed this. He knew this. By taking up residence in palaces, by ruling from them, he attached himself to the monarchic tradition and to traditional concepts of power. Tito's education and aspirations were not cultivated or refined—if one wipes them clean of the scum of Marxist teaching about class power and the withering away of the state. Essentially, he held primitive ideas about the ruler as being a caring master, the people as faithful subjects. To him, palaces, an elitist life style, and comforts reinforced the impression of power. After the war, Tito was receiving expressions of loyalty from people who had not exactly been involved in the revolution. In private, he argued with puritans like me: "The best citizens are obedient citizens. The state rests on the loyalty of its citizens."

But Tito's luxuries were incomparably more significant as an illustration of how he subjugated the Party to himself, and introduced into the Communist Party the cult of universal adulation of his personality. To be precise, he fused ideology with his personality. Tito was not the ideologist that Lenin was. He was not, as I have said, equal as an ideologist to Stalin. That fusion of ideology and personality could be achieved only through the splendor of authority. Unlike Stalin or Mao, Tito was never modest, never ordinary. Pomp was indispensable to him. It satisfied his strong *nouveau riche* instincts; it also compensated for his ideological deficiency, his inadequate education.

Splendor was the visible and drastic expression not only of Tito's intentions and ambitions, but also of the development of the Party and the government. During the war, his love of luxury and desire for power were strengthened after decisive bloody battles and legitimized by both a spontaneous and an organized popularization of Tito. It actually started before the war, when ideological Party unity was won through fierce internal struggles and class conflicts, when Tito invested his energies with persistence and guile to achieve leadership.

Of course, this appropriation of splendor had broad antiroyalist and revolutionary implications. The symbols, the seats of the monarchy, were appropriated, although the King was not formally deposed. All Communists supported Tito in this, as did others dissatisfied with the monarchy and the old Yugoslavia. What a paradox! The consciousness of Communists was still predominantly egalitarian, "of the people"; their habits and ways of life were almost ascetic. Many Communists, especially the revolutionary intellectuals who embraced ideology more literally and idealistically than most, were unable or unwilling to accept such glittering displays of power, such an inordinate appetite for luxury.

Different motives provoked the first grumblings. Early in 1945, Hebrang, who was himself given to luxury, complained to the Soviet leaders that Tito was more interested in repairing the White Palace than in the Srem military front. More often the dissatisfaction was prompted by an analogy with royalty: "Well, Tito is not a king!" The grumbling subsided quickly, because the Axis enemy was still strong and energetic; because within the Party and in his relations with the Soviets, Tito was so well established that he could wipe anyone out simply by branding him an enemy; and because his appropriation of the palaces was approved by the irrefutable authority of Moscow. The reasoning was: What can you do? The state will last; it ought to be looked after and strengthened. Tito led us while we were in prison and during the revolution. No one is without human weakness.

In taking over the royal property, Josip Broz Tito acted openly and consistently. He made it clear in little ways, as well as in his daily conversation, that whatever belonged to the court now belonged to him. That had its good side: the buildings were restored, the furniture preserved, the china, decorative objects, and works of art properly tended to. With the liberation of the country, royal properties continued to be appropriated, even those Tito could make use of only occasionally—a half-destroyed villa on Romanija Mountain, villas in Split. Moreover, the vast estates and hunting preserves of Karadjordjevo and Belje, which had been the property of the state in the old Yugoslavia, available to the royal family only for hunting parties or brief holidays, now fell under the direction and use of the new master. True, Tito showed a certain flexibility: he invited members of the Politburo and his closest associates to hunt there, especially when he was able to join them, and he made the produce grown on the estates available to them.

The only exceptions to Tito's policy of appropriation were the royal estate and villa at Topola, in Serbia, and the Queen's palace at Miločer, on the Montenegrin coast. He felt ill at ease with the former because, I believe, the burial crypt of the royal dynasty is located in the chapel there. Anyway, Topola is small, two tiny villas really, and Tito dragged around with him a large retinue of administrative and security personnel. Also, Topola is one of the most powerful and venerated shrines in the Serbian national consciousness. So it was relinquished to the Serbian government. Miločer was remote, also small. After a period of indecision—and because of Tito's preference for Brioni—it was placed at the disposal of the Montenegrin government.

As for the royal palaces in the center of Belgrade, one contained an art gallery, the other had been destroyed in an air raid. They were unsuitable for Tito, not sufficiently isolated and inadequately equipped for security. Both were restored and assigned to the federal government and the Serbian Presidium.

What was the cost of maintaining these palaces and villas, with their well-paid staffs and personnel, who themselves enjoyed certain privileges? In time, with the elimination of stockpiling of food and the introduction of the market economy, some account of Tito's expenses began to be kept —some record, at least, of staff salaries. Tito's own salary was negligible, symbolic, barely sufficient to cover food and clothing. His personal expenses were inseparable from those of the state. Building costs and the expenses of refurbishment were charged to a special state account, and Tito simply ordered the Ministry of Finance to make the payments. In lavish and privileged spending, it is impossible to distinguish the indispensable from the dispensable, or determine actual costs.

Without doubt, Tito was the most extravagant ruler of his time. It is worth remembering that King Alexander Karadjordjević—even non-Communist sources commented on this—was second only to the Japanese Emperor in his personal privileges. Officially, as regards his salary, the cost of maintaining Tito was smaller than the cost of maintaining the King, but in actuality, given the expenses necessary to maintain the staff and personnel of his estates, it was certainly larger. Tito's appropriation of luxuries hurt the Communists more than anything else. They placed themselves in a subservient position, that of courtiers, kind and loyal subjects.

Within the ranks of Tito's staff, petty issues arose. Pilfering, intrigues, and jealousy were reported. Tito never ceased to be amazed: "Unbelievable! How corrupt people around me have become!" Of course, not everyone was corrupted. There are always modest and honest people, but some were corrupted by their privileged position, even a few who under normal circumstances would not have succumbed. They were corrupted by their proximity to the power they served, by the arbitrary opportunities this offered them. It is impossible to determine what was excessive or lawless or perverse. It went beyond Tito. It was far more extensive. But Tito was at the center. Tito was the visible entity.

As Tito himself had appropriated royal wealth, he could not prevent other leading comrades from taking over the wealth of compromised political figures and the compromised rich—"compromised" here being taken loosely. During those first few years, we Communists at the top moved from villa to villa; we moved often and easily; we ordered objects from state storage, furnishings and paintings the value of which we rarely assessed. In this respect the most restrained were Koča Popović and Alexander Ranković—the former because of his intellectual puritanism, the latter because of his Party responsibilities. When it came to works of art, I also showed restraint. I immediately turned over my paintings to the National Museum and I gave a Renaissance sculpture to the Kultura bookstore. I do not know whether the paintings are still in the vaults of the museum, but to this day the sculpture stands in the middle of the bookstore.

Soon after the liberation of Belgrade, special stores were set up on the Soviet model, closed to the public and restricted to the use of higher officials. In Belgrade, the famous diplomatic store offered quality goods at token prices to government officials, Central Committee members, and the diplomatic corps.

Taking over property, moving from residence to residence, remodeling our offices, expropriating *objets d'art,* and commissioning specially designed furniture assumed the proportions of a comfortable disease. It infected not only high officials, but institutions as well. With few exceptions, luxury hotels and villas were transformed into restricted recreational centers. The Central Committee for Communist Youth had at its disposal a villa near Belgrade—allegedly used for writing reports!

I never heard Tito rebuke anyone at the top for spending lavishly on celebrations for which the cost had to be borne by the state. Needless to say, he deplored theft, corruption, and public excess of any kind. When Kidrič and I—with minor resistance from some comrades who spent the summer with Tito at Brioni—took the initiative of closing down the special stores, Tito adjusted to the change. He then separated his personal household expenses from those of the state, and concluded of domestic expenses: "Unbelievable! How much was squandered here! They just carried away whatever they wanted! One can live comfortably on one's salary." When such was the state of affairs in Tito's kitchen at 15 Užička Street, how much must have been wasted and stolen at the villas and hunting lodges and at Brioni? Tito's personal chauffeur, Prlja, a Partisan from Podgorica, who was a typical mixture of fighter and *Lumpenproletariat,* climbed the ladder of promotion so quickly that he treated both Politburo members and state property with disrespect. He was caught selling tires and spare parts from Tito's well-stocked garage, and, unable to face the scandal and imprisonment, he killed himself.

The Prlja affair, as well as Tito's decision to separate his personal household expenses from those of the state, occurred in the early fifties, at the height of the struggle against bureaucratism and Stalinism. However, with the renewed consolidation of Tito's personal power, personal and official expenses once again became hopelessly entangled. The property and vineyards of a gentleman farmer, Mosek, came under the direct control of the new palace, and soon became a principal source of foodstuffs. The peasants referred to that estate as "Tito's homestead." Nor did they

think that strange—once it was Mosek's, now it was Tito's.
Early on, Party bureaucrats referred to executive headquarters as "the court"; later it was referred to more appro-
priately as the "Marshal's headquarters."

The most extensive building was done on the island of
Brioni, Tito's summer residence. It retained the stamp of
its original owner, in the days of the Austro-Hungarian
Empire. Tito put in a zoo; he liked to have game bred for
him and he liked to hunt it down. A hotel for high government and Party officials was built, with everything of the
finest quality. At first, Tito took up residence in the villa
of the Duke of Spoleto, which he later generously handed
over to Kardelj, when he erected a new and spacious villa
for himself. "You'll be able to hold a reception for five
hundred here," he boasted while the villa was being built.
The construction at the island was largely done by prisoners—admittedly they were better off than in prison and
had better prospects for pardon or parole.

In 1952 or 1953, when I had already begun to express my
"anarcholiberalism," Svetozar Vukmanović-Tempo came
back from a visit to Brioni and told me that Tito had
jokingly said: "Tell Djido what my villa is like, and tell
him all that is great in history was built by slaves." I never
went to Brioni except for official purposes. This was noticed, and I was reproached: "You are sticking out from the
collective."

At Belje, next to the royal hunting lodge, Tito put up an
authentic hunting château. He did the same elsewhere: he
would not consent to stay in houses that were not his except
for a short time, and then grudgingly. At Igalo, where he
went to the thermal baths to relieve his sciatica, a hill was
razed. It had been part of a municipal park. He was said
not to be quite happy with the villa at Igalo, and work was

begun on a new one at Miločer, adjacent to the small palace of the Queen. Tito was then eighty-five or eighty-six.

He was fussy when it came to furnishing the palaces and villas and acquiring works of art. Sometimes he would pick things out himself, other times they would be selected for him by officials, who thereby affirmed their loyalty and improved their standing. The sculptor Antun Avgustinčić's "Venera of Brioni" was acquired in this manner and sent as a "gift" to Tito's villa at Brioni. Most of the paintings that the collector Mimara bequeathed to the "Croatian people" after the war, to the national museums of Croatia, ended up in Tito's villa in Zagreb.

I must sound like an *enfant terrible* in the Yugoslav leadership of that period, because I spotted everything and alerted everyone to everything. And it is true that in 1946 or 1947, when Tito was showing off to a group of functionaries the newly arrived paintings from Mimara's collection, I did say: "These should be given to the museums." No one echoed my view. Tito snapped back: "You don't know what the state is. We keep art here for show. Besides, it's better cared for here." Twenty years later, a scandal erupted: through the foreign press, Mimara asked where the paintings were. As a result, the paintings were finally brought together in the museums.

Some of what happened was absurd. The royal train was inherited, too, but the royal train was not comfortable or plush enough for Tito. He ordered it remodeled. Two armored cars were added to the train, one at the front and one at the rear. The Soviets advised us on such fundamental security measures at the end of the war. That was before their systematic recruitment of our officials and employees assumed its sinister aspect.

Tito acted like a poor man who seized the opportunity

to acquire, to build, to improve. Consciously and unconsciously for him, the present blended with the future; he sought continuity in buildings. He often said: "One should build. Something always remains." But he did not build alone. Others built for him—officials from the republics and the provinces, with his consent, of course. In 1952 Djuro Pucar, President of the Bosnian government, explained to me why a palace was constructed on Vrelo Bosne: "We built it for the Old Man—when he turns up in Sarajevo." Often such enterprises were undertaken not only to please Tito. Some were probably built with that pretext, but for the use of local officials as well. Did Tito know how many palaces were at his disposal? I doubt that anyone knew. Many palaces and villas were built for him to satisfy regional and local appetites and pretensions.

Tito accepted gifts with the utmost seriousness. A Rolls-Royce was a "tribute from the city of Zagreb," said Tito. The villas that Pavelić confiscated from the Jews, the people of Zagreb later handed over to Tito, who called them "homage from the city of Zagreb," as if the people of Zagreb did it from the goodness of their hearts.

Tito's apparatus and many federal and regional bureaucracies appropriated major hunting preserves. The best hunting grounds, those abundant with game, were chiefly federal property. At that time, a joke was making the rounds that only rabbits were regional or local game.

Two hunts stand out in my memory, each indelible, each significant regarding the revolution and my heretical stance toward Tito.

States with common borders usually quarrel more often than families living next door. The Serbs and the Romanians are an exception, having never quarreled. Even though

Antonescu did not close his air bases to the Germans, the Romanian Army did not engage in military actions against Yugoslavia. The new Yugoslavia and the new Romania have inherited a long-standing friendship. The war was not yet over when Petru Groza, the Romanian President, came to visit Tito. It was the first visit of a neighboring head of state. Like us, the Romanians had had a tough time. They suffered in the knowledge that they had allowed their Party and their resistance movement practically to be extinguished. They appreciated us more than we appreciated them, for they saw the great Serbian uprisings of the past as a harbinger of the revolutionary Yugoslav war against fascism.

One day, the Romanians invited our leader to a hunting party. There was pretension on both sides—at a hunting party, rulers and statesmen confirm cordiality and good intentions. Among the Communist leaders in Eastern Europe —and the Yugoslavs no doubt took the lead—hunting feasts were manifestations of power. None of us, not even Tito, had been hunters before the war. (As an adolescent I had enjoyed fishing.) We went hunting less to relax than to exhibit our power and our prestige. I do not remember where that state hunting party took place. It could not have been too far from the border. The hunt was scheduled for the next day—at dawn, of course.

That evening, Romanian officials included Gheorghe Gheorghiu-Dej, the Party Secretary, and Anna Pauker, who was superficial, but beautiful despite her advanced years. Visile Luka gave a dinner party in the royal castle. Petru Groza, who had been a landowner in Transylvania, did not attend the dinner. He had been prime minister under King Michael and must have felt uncomfortable attending feasts in royal castles. Nor did he join the hunt the following day. Dressed in a riding habit, he merely strolled about, smiling enigmatically.

The dinner was lavish, replete with Romanian specialties that reminded us of our national dishes. There were Romanian gypsies, who sang passionately and played their pipes expertly. With conversation and pleasantries, the dinner stretched into the small hours of the morning. The next day our security men told us that the royal family was staying in that very same castle, confined to one room on the upper floor. The castle had been their sanctuary while King Michael was in exile. We were uncomfortable. I felt like a member of a refined gang of robbers. Still, we could not help but be amused by this Romanian indiscretion. We were even more amused when we learned that the Romanian security men had searched the gypsies, and retrieved from them the silver of the royal family, stolen while we were enjoying the food and wine and music.

A second discovery we made ourselves during the hunt. Koča Popović was the first to observe that the beaters—there were several hundred of them—did not look like peasants, though they wore fur hats and sheepskin coats. They were young and delicate, with fair complexions. What was most extraordinary was that there were girls among them. We chatted with them. They held back at first, but bit by bit they opened up. They were students, most of them Party members, who had been brought in by bus all the way from Bucharest. They all spoke French. They felt silly, but they had been curious to see Tito.

Another hunting party revealed the quality of relationships at the very top in our own government. I did not participate in that hunt. It took place in September 1953. Tito and other leaders were in Belje. Kardelj had just finished work on the new constitutional law that was to replace the Constitution of 1946, modeled in many ways on the Stalin Constitution of 1936. Kardelj attached great importance to the new law, because he saw it as an instrument that would facilitate the process of democratization. When people had earlier pointed out to him that the National Assembly resembled a morgue, with delegates raising their hands like puppets, he responded reassuringly. "Now there is going to be plenty of discussion—the hard questions will be decided here." He even went so far as to say to me mischievously: "Maybe we shall gradually arrive at an opposition." According to the new law, the president would be chief of state, taking over the role of the Presidium. Tito was, of course, expected to assume that function. While the law was still being drafted, Kardelj described it at a meeting of the Politburo or the Central Committee Secretariat. Tito aggressively addressed himself to the particular aspects of the rights and role of the president. Kardelj had anticipated that and magnified the functions of the president to accommodate Tito's pretensions. After that, it seemed that the law would meet with no obstacles.

The constitutional law reflected our vigorous championing—opposite from the deviations of Stalin and the Soviets —of Marx's teaching about the withering away of the proletarian state. At that time, Kardelj was probably the most consistent and the most prominent and respected theoretician. He combined the concept of the withering away of the state with democratization and self-management. He believed that if the Party had too much influence in everyday life, especially in economic life, it obstructed the process of democratization and self-management. The constitutional law therefore provided for a government composed of professionals—Communists, of course—and for the transfer of the top Partisan officials to the National Assembly as deputies, thereby strengthening the role and the standing of the Assembly. Tito was familiar with Kardelj's position, as well as with the provisions in the constitutional law that supported this change. So it was assumed that the change was acceptable.

But, as luck would have it, Kardelj was promptly summoned to Belje, where Tito was hunting deer. Kardelj stayed only overnight—he wasn't exactly up to hunting. At that time, I saw Kardelj almost daily or had long telephone conversations with him—not to discuss affairs of state, mainly, but to exchange ideas. We had a lot in common. That is how I knew that he had gone to Belje. I had a premonition that something unpleasant would happen, because that summer at the meeting of the Central Committee Plenum at Brioni, Tito had already begun to restrain the process of democratization, and to return the Party to the tested straight paths of Leninist-Stalinist theory.

I showed up at Kardelj's office the day after his return from Belje. He told me: "The Old Man said: 'All of you [that is to say, the top Party officials] can go to the National Assembly, but leave me here alone!' " That meant that Tito was not favorably inclined toward a government composed of professionals. He was most decidedly against the Central Committee members joining the National Assembly. He was obviously wary of the strenthened role of the Assembly under the leadership of the top Party officials. I did not approve of Tito's rejection of this constitutional law, because I believed, perhaps naïvely, that the law as drafted provided for the democratization of the top echelons of the government. Above all, I was offended by the way Tito objected—without consulting the Politburo, and during a hunt. Clearly, he did not consider it urgent enough to justify a return to Belgrade.

I believed, mistakenly perhaps—or maybe I was under the spell of heresy already—that such decision-making and the manner in which Kardelj was summoned were not accidental. Tito was forcefully and drastically reestablishing relations at the top as they had existed before the confrontation with Stalin and the subsequent reforms. Those had been modest, secondary reforms, which were, if nothing else, important symbolically, in my view. I reproached Kardelj: "You were summoned and you went!" "It's not exactly like that!" Kardelj retorted, stung, offended because I had recognized his subservient relationship with Tito—probably offended more by that than he was ashamed of the relationship itself.

I think it was around that time that I said to Kardelj: "Tito is the standard-bearer of bureaucracy!" Kardelj quoted that statement at the Third Plenum, in January 1954, of the Central Committee, at which I was condemned for revisionism and dismissed from the Central Committee. Why did Kardelj do that? Perhaps more out of disloyalty to me personally, and political opportunism, than out of fear that our conversation had been bugged. Most likely both reasons were at work.

Nothing is picked up more easily, nothing adjusted to more quickly, than the life of luxury. Where there is power, there are always hangers-on who manage to smooth the way for you. So it was with us, toward the end of the war, as we began to climb the ladder of power. And so it was with Tito. In those first years there was clumsiness and primitivism, more with some than with others, depending on one's cultural background and one's ingenuity. Tito adapted most readily, but because of his position and his pretensions, he found himself in the most complex and delicate situation. In his palaces and villas, order was promptly established on a European level. If the staff slipped up, out of either ignorance or lack of culture, its behavior was quickly corrected. Tito's court was in no way inferior to the royal court that had preceded it; in ostentation, it surpassed its predecessor. It was natural for Tito to parade his jewelry, to indulge in pomp. It had nothing to do with his staff or with protocol. His uniforms were edged with gold. Everything that he used had to be just right and very special. His belt buckle was made out of pure gold, and was so heavy that it kept slipping down. He wrote with a heavy gold pen. His chair was impressive and always placed at the center of the room. He changed his clothes as often as four times a day, according to the occasion and the impressions he wished to create. In the presence of the army leaders, he wore the uniform of a marshal. When he turned up in military uniform among civilians, or with Central Committee members, that might mean he wished to convey the idea that, whatever the issue at hand, he had the army behind him. He used a sun lamp regularly to maintain a tan. His hair was dyed, his teeth were false and gleaming white. Though he was naturally vigorous, in public appearances he often made a special effort to be animated and high-spirited.

Tito worked hard to develop a style. Others worked hard to keep pace with that style. Style and substance eventually became one. I think that the way he shook hands changed after 1944, when he was installed in Belgrade; afterward, his hand hung slackly by his side, so those who shook it were forced to bow slightly.

Tito also fought for his style, drawing on the resourcefulness of his subordinates. For example, he wanted our newspapers to publish his telegrams to foreign statesmen marking special events. This posed a serious problem. In the prewar press, such telegrams were rarely published. Nor was this the custom followed elsewhere in the world, not even in Stalin's Russia. So our editors published Tito's telegrams in inconspicuous spots in their newspapers, often not at all. The Cabinet intervened, and Tito himself said to me a few times: "That ruins my reputation!" I hardly thought so, but I interceded and the situation improved. Then some assistant editor blundered, leading to more Cabinet intervention and more anger from Tito. This went on for several years, until Vladimir Dedijer was appointed editor in chief of the Party newspaper, *Borba*. "I've solved the problem of Tito's telegrams. We'll print them on the front page." And so, instead of the customary editorials on major issues, the front page presented us with telegrams of greetings to and from Tito—which no one bothered to read, because they were indistinguishable from one another.

Collecting medals for Tito was a high priority in state politics. At home, the medals marked various national anniversaries and achievements in which he had played a prominent role. The exchange of medals with visiting foreign dignitaries became an obligatory courtesy. Once upon a time, there was a Montenegrin king, Nikola I, who was fond of medals, but Tito outdid him and was second to none. He held one of the largest collections of medals in history. How deeply his passion for medals has permeated the national consciousness was demonstrated most dramatically by the recent proposal of a Belgrade branch of the Socialist Alliance (the National Front) that Tito be awarded the Fourth Order of the National Hero for endurance—in this instance, for a successful surgical operation. That proposal was quietly abandoned when complications set in during the course of Tito's last illness.

Demonstrations of public tribute to Tito were never spontaneous—roughly speaking, the more spontaneous they seemed, the less spontaneous they were. During the war, and immediately following it, revolutionary enthusiasm was mixed with fear of defeat. Gradually, those two elements dissolved into ritualistic, conformist celebrations full of pomp and ceremony. With shifts in the leadership, familiar faces gradually disappeared from posters and public display, except for Tito's. Absolute personal power inevitably leads to the impersonal.

The issue of how to celebrate May Day caused the members of the Agitprop of the Central Committee, and particularly me, its director, no end of grief. In the beginning there was a genuine spontaneity in those celebrations, as there was in the festivities that marked Tito's birthday. Spontaneity is pleasant and attractive, but not powerful or arresting. Gradually, organization took over. Zogović did not like these staged spectacles of cheering tribute and parades of homage. He said to me at the May Day parade in 1946, satirizing a medical-surgical unit demonstrating an operation on top of a truck: "Next time they'll demonstrate a delivery!"

As the organizational structure of celebrations grew, so did complaints, right there on the grandstand and later at Politburo meetings. A separate body organized demonstrations, but Agitprop was in charge, so I was under fire. The criticism, however, was petty: Why did you have a poster of this leader and not that one? Why are some posters smaller than others? Why was this factory's display such a mess? Why do those suburbanites march like slobs, while the downtown crowds are all nicely aligned? Why is Stalin's

picture smaller (or bigger) than Tito's? Tito complained
the least, perhaps because every unit in the parade cheered
him and carried his picture—bigger and better than the
rest, except for Stalin's! Yet Kardelj, Ranković, and others
goaded Tito into passing final judgment on matters to which
he was essentially indifferent. All these details were important when it came to maintaining relations at the top, and
consequently, by God, important for the country and the
people! Agitprop was on top of things: drawing on past
experience, we approached the problem with renewed vigor.
At the meeting of the Politburo, I made a proposal (and
with certain amendments my proposal was accepted) spec-
ifying the number of posters to be used in the May Day
celebration, of which leaders and how large, how many
thousands of citizens should attend (the figure did not have
to be exact), how many floats, how many, how much, all
down the line. That brought an end to both criticism and
spontaneity, from the top and from the bottom. The issue
of the May Day parade was finally settled, until the parades
themselves began to peter out, mainly owing to the widen-
ing ideological rift with the Soviet Union.

In the formation of this style, Tito relied a good deal on
imitation. He invented nothing. And imitation was the
bone that stuck in people's throats most of all and provoked
criticism and confidential complaints, even within Tito's
immediate circle. In royalist Yugoslavia, there was a custom
that the monarch became godfather to the ninth boy in any
family. The tradition originated in Serbia as a tribute to
the fabled nine Jugović brothers, who fell in the fateful
Battle of Kosovo in 1389. Tito appropriated the custom as
soon as he installed himself in the royal palaces. But it was
impossible for him to assume the godfather's duties im-
plicit in that royal act. To begin with, there was no reli-

gious service; moreover, the fourteenth century had not anticipated the equality of men and women. But godfathering was godfathering, even in the absence of a priest and without baptism—no one was able to come up with a substitute for that word, and it was applied even to a female child. There were quite a lot of families with nine children. Some even began to claim their right retroactively, and to ask for and receive from this most famous and powerful godfather all kinds of benefits and privileges. So Tito's godfathering proliferated and dragged on for two decades— until he got fed up with it.

Tito's imitation of the horse-racing customs of the rich was so shocking and grotesque that it upset his close circle —Kardelj and Ranković, among others. As soon as horse racing was permitted again, references were heard to "horses from Marshal Tito's stable." The stables had been nationalized and were the property of the state. Then it turned out that there was still one private stable left—that single exception was the private stable of Marshal Tito. It was common knowledge, though, that he was not particularly interested in horses, and that Marshal Tito's stable was actually a military horse-breeding ranch. Still, the Marshal's stable won far too often! What would have happened if there had been gambling casinos? The newspapers were perplexed: the word came from the race track that this or that horse from the stable of Marshal Josip Broz Tito had won, and from Tito's Cabinet came the order that the news item be published. Possibly the confidential reports of the secret police (which arrived from all regions daily and which Tito read avidly) were unfavorable, and the adverse comments from the top too frequent. A year or two later, the horses from the stable of Marshal Tito stopped winning.

It had been the royal custom, most often observed by the

Queen, to donate gifts to orphanages. However, the former crowned heads did not give excessively—perhaps because what they gave came out of their own pockets—nor did they travel often or pay many visits to orphanages. But Tito traveled a lot and he frequently visited orphanages, which the war had made so plentiful. And the money? For Tito, money was never an object; he simply gave orders that it be dispensed out of the state's treasury, always in new bills, neatly counted and stacked. Those at the receiving end were invariably pleased, but perplexed. They knew that Tito was not giving out of his own pocket: was aid given simply because Tito happened to drop by?

Perhaps the most embarrassing incident, for the recipients as well as for us, his accomplices, took place on Tito's trip to Montenegro in the summer of 1946. We stopped at Užice to visit an orphanage. After the director of the orphanage was handed the money, she simply stood there, stunned. She stuttered: "We have enough money. Other orphanages are much worse off than we are. Much worse. Thank you." When we returned to Belgrade, Ranković and I discussed Tito's imitation of royalty. Ranković did not support me in my criticism, but he did not report me either. On the question of monetary gifts—surely because he himself had been witness to unpleasant scenes of charity—he commented: "I don't approve of that. It's unjust and degrading." Yet that custom was perpetuated until Tito finally realized that by mimicking the charity of kings, he was diminishing his own reputation.

Kings are people like any other. Few become leaders and autocrats. Along with their crowns, kings inherit a code of courtly etiquette. Few of them know how to rule royally, as absolute monarchs. Many kings might envy Tito his absolute power—and some did. Yet, because he was a subtle and gifted politician, he did not establish a dynasty. After all, had not the nation just renounced one king? Tito had no need for the crown. He also could not establish a single-person succession, a crown prince.

10

It is impossible to separate Tito's private life from his political activity. I have no wish to intrude on any person's intimate life, but Tito was not "any person." Even in moments of relaxation, the political Tito was always present. He sought to integrate his private and public personalities, but when they collided, politics invariably won. Could it have been otherwise?

I would break the thread of my analytical study if I did not attempt to assess, at least to describe, the interplay of Tito's private and public personalities. It is extremely difficult to describe this connection in a political leader, though the connection is deeper and stronger and more significant than objective Marxist theory would have it.

Josip Broz Tito was a spirited, somewhat nervous, but controlled person. His hands were blunt but wiry. They matched the strong bone structure of his face. When he gained weight after the Fifth Offensive, in 1943, his hands became pudgy. From a compelling calm he would abruptly spring into motion, his hands reaching out, his face full of expression. His deep-set blue eyes would open wide and gleam under the arch of fair brows. But he would check that sudden animation just as suddenly, and his demeanor would revert to its usual state, self-satisfied, but anxious, and rarely peaceful. Tito could be sensitive and compassionate, given to delight; also, he could yield to spurts of anger and great uneasiness. Quickly and boldly, he would retrieve himself from uncertainty and plunge headlong into action. The weaknesses of Tito's military strategy, as a commander in the field, reflected this temperament, but this disposition was an advantage, too, especially in making strategic political decisions.

Tito was an energetic man with a sturdy physical constitution. He never complained about physical stress; nor did he shrink from physical exertions. He did not have to muster—as so many did, I among them—all his strength in a show of confidence to keep up the morale of our men. On a night march over Prenj Mountain in March 1943, during the Fourth Offensive, Tito found himself without a horse. He had to push himself strenuously to keep up on foot, but he made it to the front lines, setting such a fast pace for the rank and file that they griped and swore, unaware who was egging them on. In marching with Tito, this kind of rush was more or less the norm. And that rush revealed his physical endurance and energy—nervous energy, which fed incessantly on itself but seemed to control itself instinctively. As with Stalin, Tito's power of concentration was formidable. But Stalin's was disguised by a frail body, and emerged only through the sharpness of his mind and his facial expression. Tito's concentration was reflected in his whole body.

Tito was an exceptionally handsome man—more so to women than to men. He was fair, tanned, solidly built. His head was round, his forehead high, his nose slightly curved, his lips thin, his jaw strong. The vitality of his movements, the concentrated force of his compact body, and especially his nervous energy made him striking on first sight. He was somewhat Germanic or Nordic in appearance. Avgustinčić, who made several busts of Tito, used to joke: "He must have noble blood in him. Whoever saw such a man from Zagorje?" (Zagorje is the heart of old Croatia.) A certain Yugoslav admiral once wrote that it was not unimportant that our leader was, above all, handsome. Perhaps he didn't know that all men look handsome to their admirers when they become leaders. However, objectively, in all fairness, one can say that Tito was truly a remarkably handsome man.

Tito was passionate, direct. Passionate in everything—food and drink, love and hate, decision-making. Passionate in the most crucial affairs and the most petty. He sometimes lost control in critical situations, but not for long. In fact, he allowed himself to lose control only when he thought that it would work to his political advantage. When you heard "Tito is angry!" it generally meant that the issue at hand had better be removed from the agenda.

Soon after I first met Tito, in Zagreb in the spring of 1937, he scheduled a secret meeting in the mountains above Sevnica, in Slovenia. He stayed in a nearby hotel with a young woman courier named Herta Hass. She in time became his wife. It did not occur to Kardelj, Lola Ribar, and others to take along their female companions, even as a measure to divert the authorities. Tito behaved as if there was no distinction between his love life and important Party business. But he excluded Herta from the meeting. He sent her to the railway station to meet our comrades from Ljubljana. I recall that Tito was enthusiastic about the chicken soup, but disappointed with the bad weather, and quickly distracted from both by the important tasks at hand.

Quite naturally, Tito's passionate nature was visible during the war—in countless desperate efforts to survive, to win. His telegrams to the Comintern reflected the divisions and discords between the Yugoslav revolution and Soviet interests, as they did Tito's personality. His tone, the vehemence of his disagreement, particularly when it came to the Soviet's ambivalence regarding the collaboration of Draža Mihailović's Chetniks with the occupation forces, often exceeded the limits prescribed for Communists in their relations with Moscow. Tito gained stature in Moscow's eyes with the consolidation of our army, and from our growing prestige in the West and our pivotal position in the Balkans. But there was bad blood between Moscow and Belgrade during the war because of the unprecedented efforts of the Yugoslav leaders to shape the image and the position of the Yugoslav revolution. What armed struggle is not a struggle for power? Such was Tito's impassioned nature that he suffered intensely over human massacres and human misery. But under the pressure of new responsibilities, the same nature gave way to its customary activity, neither humane nor inhumane, simply life-enhancing and life-accepting.

Tito's companionship was pleasant except when it came to political experience. He had a sense of humor, certainly, although his jokes were not imaginative or original. Neither were they crude or insulting. He could make a joke at his own expense—the milder kind, jokes not directed at his prestige or his vanity. I do not recall that he ever made a joke at Kardelj's expense, nor did Kardelj at his. Relations between them were sober, businesslike, though close. Ranković joked with Tito warmly, but cautiously. The other comrades were careful, too: Tito was older, had greater responsibilities, and could be touchy. Generally speaking, those of us at the top were not crude in our dealings with each other: our long association, our various friendships, as well as the hardships and responsibilities we shared, made casual insults a cause for sorrow rather than for anger. Tito laughed wholeheartedly at a well-told joke, sometimes to the point of tears. He would shout, "Go to the Devil!" and continue laughing, his body heaving with amusement.

Tito did not swear, except to express his contempt for the enemy. Even then he used only folk phrases devoid of expletives. Nor did the other comrades swear. The exception was Moša Pijade, whose cursing was in his blood, a linguistic and emotional heritage from Dorćol, a Belgrade suburb. He swore irresistibly, with joy and passion. We enjoyed his cursing, no one reproached him for it, for there was no official position on that.

In his free time, while traveling on trains, on his hunting trips, or on unofficial visits, Tito enjoyed random conversation, or a game of dominoes or chess—chess less often, because it required much time and concentration. He played dominoes absent-mindedly. The domino pieces lay flat on the table in front of him, and with every move he would pick up the pieces and examine them. He never gambled. There was no gambling among the top leadership, although it caught on later, years after the revolution.

Tito was, on the whole, talkative, though less so in private than in public. He rarely spoke about himself. It annoyed him when others talked on and on. He liked to stick to specifics and usually was open and reasonable. But if a question embarrassed him, he would brush it aside curtly: "That can't be helped. One does not talk about such things. You want information that doesn't exist."

In mortal danger Tito kept a certain distance, became impenetrable and inaccessible. Between him and his friends, and his wives, there was always a movable barrier. A movable barrier, not a gulf! The barrier was moved instinctively. You could see it closing whenever anyone got too close—a certain hardening in his expression, a flicker of malice in his eyes. Tito was not made for confessions or empathy. His entire being announced without ambiguity: I am I, and you are you, and I am exceptional. He was serious, responsible, and self-confident.

Tito had a good memory but not a long one. For example, he never retaliated against Kardelj, who did not uphold him in his June 5, 1945, exchange with the Soviet Ambassador, Ivan Sadchikov. Tito knew that a public break with Kardelj would be advantageous to Stalin and damaging to his own position. Besides, Kardelj was punished enough when the meeting with Sadchikov was made public. Tito never forgot affronts to his pride and vanity. He considered pride to be the basic characteristic of the Yugoslav people, simply because he himself was defiant.

On one occasion, shortly before my break with Tito, I observed that Austria did not enforce denationalization. "True," Tito remarked. "Austria makes sure that Austrians come first. The reason I didn't become a fencing champion in the Austrian Army was simply that I was a Croat." In this connection, it was reported that on his last visit to Austria, Tito was willing to accept an Austrian medal that had been awarded him during World War I.

Tito's impulse to identify himself with history was kindled by his vanity, which ranged from pettiness to megalomania. He jealously guarded every trinket in his possession,

Tito in 1944 at his headquarters
in the Yugoslav mountains

UP

Tito's birthplace in Kumrovec

Tito (top left) as a metalworker at age nineteen

Sipa / Black Sta

Photograph of Tito taken in jail in 1928
following the bomb-squad trial

Tito with his secretary, Zdenka, in Montenegro in 1943

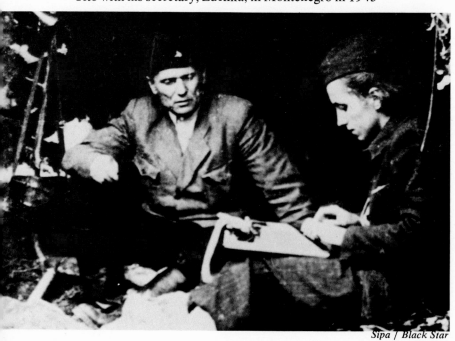

Antun Avgustinčić sculpting a bust of Tito in 1943

The Partisan leadership in Vis, summer 1944.
Left to right: Vladimir Bakarić, Ivan Milutinović,
Edvard Kardelj, Josip Broz Tito, Alexander-Leka Ranković,
Svetozar Vukmanović-Tempo, and Milovan Djilas

Tito signing the Soviet-Yugoslav agreement in Moscow in 1944,
with Molotov, on the right, standing next to Stalin

Tito, Djilas (far right) and Ranković (second from left)
with a village delegation in 1944

Tito and his wife, Jovanka, at Brioni in 1957

Tito's official residence on the island
of Brioni and his private launch

Tito reviewing Victory Day Parade in Belgrade in 1975

Tito at seventy

Tito's family—sons Miša and Žarko with Jovanka
—at Tito's funeral in May 1980

and at the same time encouraged and supervised the construction of monuments and museums dedicated to himself.
Tito was not a spendthrift. His luxury was calculated. But
he was possessive, particularly when it came to objects that
served him. They had to bear his imprint. In the courtyard
of his villa on Užička Street, he installed a bronze statue of
his horse.

Tito had really loved this horse, which had served him
during the war. Somehow or other, after the war, the horse
was brought to Belgrade, where Tito had a stable built for
it in his garden. That same horse was a cause of Žujović's
hostility to Tito. After the attack on Drvar of May 25, 1944,
Tito had to fly to Italy. As he boarded the plane, he called
out to Žujović: "Take care of my horse!" Žujović was furi-
ous. "He's worried about his horse, and we are in this hell-
hole!" Žujović, who was less vain and more heroic than
Tito, just couldn't understand this trait. Tito loved his
soldiers. He loved his horse, too.

In the garden of his villa, Tito had a storehouse constructed for the gifts piling up. That was the beginning of
the Museum of the 25th of May (the day on which Tito's
birthday is celebrated). In 1968 the new director of the
museum set out to remodel it. Tito approved the plans.

Cities, schools, factories, and streets were named after
him. There is hardly a town in all of Yugoslavia that does
not boast his name. The paths that he trod during the war,
the places where he stayed, are shrines. It is as if there were
nothing in Tito's character that was final, unalterable—as
if everything were conditional, mutable, and changing.

Tito's response to sudden hostility, it must be said, was
savage and irrational. Since he had absolute power, he sometimes went dangerously far. But usually, after initial rage,
he would subside and give consideration to reasonable alter-

natives. In 1946 hints of a rift with Hebrang and Žujović were revealed at a Central Committee meeting. Tito said: "What leaders of Yugoslavia they would make! One an Ustasha, the other a Chetnik!" (Hebrang was a Croat, Žujović was a Serb.) But when he met our icy stares—after all, Hebrang and Žujović were old-guard Communists—Tito fell silent and dropped the subject.

In March 1943 Tito made a heartfelt attempt, in which I was involved, to secure the release of his former wife, Herta, whom he had abandoned, from a German concentration camp. After the war, alone and embittered, Herta, it was said, spread stories about him all over Belgrade. He dismissed her acidly: *"Volksdeutscher!"* (Herta's parents were Austrians.) This comment met with strong disapproval. Once again, rare as it was, Tito backed off.

These two examples—one a political, Party issue, the other a personal affair—illustrate Tito's way of reacting to sudden threats. He gave importance to matters that had nothing to do with politics; he considered disagreements with him to be downright hostility. Tito absorbed something of that approach in the Soviet Union, but he bore the seed within him.

When he suspected deviation, Tito would drop hints to his associates: "What's wrong with him?" "Curious attitudes!" "He's been alienated lately!" "Have you noticed anything?" "By God, that's not accidental." After the devastating and sobering conflict with Stalin in 1948, he yielded to a more moderate position and recognized that political differences were inevitable within a movement or among friends.

Tito's guile was dictated by political expediency rather than by character. When one got to know him well, one could tell whether he was sincere or was dissembling. When he was up to something, his face would soften and break into a smile. On two occasions, he submitted his official resignation: the first time it was genuine; the second, it was a fraud. The first took place in December of 1941, in the village of Drenova, near Užice, following the First German Offensive, which left us defeated and demoralized. Tito was exhausted. Without any prompting, he offered his resignation as Party secretary. According to the memory of another Politburo member, Tito also offered to resign as supreme commander. The second occasion was his offer to resign as president of the government, on March 1, 1948, at a Politburo meeting, because of the strained relations with the Soviets following the report on the Kardelj-Djilas talks in Moscow. But it was obvious to me, as it was to other comrades, that Tito was simply testing us. Everyone was genuinely opposed to his resignation, except Žujović, who was already under suspicion and did not comment.

Tito was keenly aware that in politics one must be cunning. His shrewdness was a means of penetrating the intentions of his opponent and setting in motion counter-measures. I will cite two episodes, which no one has yet recorded. In the summer of 1948, when we were tensely uncertain about Soviet plans, I prodded Tito into speculating about what might happen. We were at Split, on the Adriatic coast. Tito exclaimed: "The Americans are not fools. They won't let the Russians reach the Adriatic." It was my impression that during the early stages of the confrontation with the Soviet Union, Tito had no contact with the American government. Relations with the United States were still strained. They had not forgotten the shooting down of their aircraft after the war and our encouragement of the civil war in Greece. Yet Tito relied on American support throughout his dispute with the Soviet Union.

I would be hypocritical if I failed to mention that, despite my ideological rejection of capitalism and the United States, I found Tito's reading of events gratifying.

During the Korean War, another crisis erupted over Berlin. Moscow and its satellites inexplicably softened their campaign against Yugoslavia, and stepped up their attacks on the United States and Western Europe. During those years, we at the top explored numerous options regarding a possible attack on us from the east—even the option of joining the Atlantic alliance. Kardelj, Ranković, and I were at Tito's villa on Užička Street when the shift in the Soviet position came up for discussion. It was suggested that the Soviet Union might launch an attack against Europe, and leave us for last. Tito was already climbing the stairs, on his way to his bedroom, when he suddenly said: "You know, I've given a lot of thought to this matter. It crossed my mind that if it comes to something like that, we should provoke an incident." It was on that occasion, I believe, that Tito quoted the time-honored adage: Politics is a great whore.

There is a widespread belief that Tito was a diligent and obsessive worker. Actually, he was not as hard-working as Kardelj, and Kardelj was not as hard-working as Ranković or Kidrič. Yet Tito was conscientious and thorough and never overlooked the slightest detail, even though he was overburdened, particularly at the beginning of his rule, when he wanted to be a man of the people and personally attend to all complaints and appeals.

His work and his life were tightly scheduled. He rose early and was usually at his desk by eight o'clock. He received visitors in the morning. He ate lunch and dinner at the same time every day. After lunch, he walked for an hour, then returned to his desk to look over reports. In the evening, after dinner, he would invariably see a film, any film if there was nothing good around. By eleven he was in bed. He put himself to sleep by reading agency reports. Even when he traveled, he kept to this routine. The schedule was disturbed only by important meetings or by a game of billiards, which he would play with his comrades until all hours of the morning. Gradually he gave up that diversion, as did the rest of us. With new family and other responsibilties, the bonds of intimacy slackened.

Tito also expressed his sense of order in his clothing and in his eating habits. For every occasion he was dressed to the hilt. His clothes were new and fashionable, not a wrinkle or a spot. During the war, he paid particular attention to his appearance. There was something *nouveau riche* in this appetite for fashion, this weakness for uniforms. Tito was moderate in food and drink. He ate well but not excessively, though he had a weakness for starches, smoked meats, especially sausages, and hearty soups—the winter dishes from his native region. In January 1941 I accompanied him on a drive from Ljubljana to Zagreb. (He owned a car then, and had a chauffeur, a Party member.) We stopped in his native village to visit his relatives, an elderly couple. He had paid them to fatten two pigs for slaughter and he asked questions about the meat. The sausages were delicious, but could have been smoked longer. As for alcohol, he took a small glass now and then, rarely two, and only in cold weather or when he was exhausted. For lunch, he had a glass or two of wine, mixed with water. It was rumored that in his last years he drank whiskey in large amounts. I doubt that. I cannot believe that he lost control or went beyond what doctors recommended.

Wherever he stayed, neatness and cleanliness were the rules of the day. That fit well with protocol and prestige.

His staff were equally tidy and clean. The chambermaids wore white uniforms, the waiters tuxedos. In the forests, during hunts, the staff were dressed formally. There was no familiarity between Tito and his servants. This regularity and precision no doubt cleared the way for contemplation. For Tito, contemplation was a necessary habit, engaged in most often during his walks. In strained or taxing moments, he strolled with his hands linked behind his back, releasing his anger and doubts to himself, or to others if anyone happened to be around.

What was Tito thinking about? Like anybody else, about whatever came to mind. Most often, I believe, Tito concentrated on specific problems. His random and lengthy contemplation was indispensable to his decision-making: for Tito, contemplation was work, difficult and exacting work. It was easier to persuade him than to dissuade him. When he fixed his mind on something, only cold, hard facts could deflect him from his course. And in discussion, he could be intolerant. At meetings involving more than two other people, he could be sharp and unpleasant, as he was not in a discussion with only one person, when the atmosphere was almost always more intimate.

Tito conducted his official tasks with dispatch. He was the essence of exactitude, a formidable and consistent opponent of verbosity. Inflexibility and intolerance derived from his authoritarian temperament, and also from the single-mindedness of his working method. Ranković was also notable for his patience and attention to detail. Kardelj was tolerant, but vague and undefined at the center. Tito's toughness and intolerance were not a liability, for in dealing with people he tended to be flexible, broad-minded, and compliant. He was obstinate and split hairs only when his prestige was concerned. That prestige was as important to him as any matter of state.

Tito rarely used the telephone for official purposes except in emergencies—when he thought he saw signs of significant political deviation, when it was a question of a serious error. For months at a time, he would not ask me to visit him; nor would I request a visit. In the meantime, there were meetings at his villa, but Tito never took advantage of them to nag or harass his subordinates. Such an approach instilled a sense of personal autonomy in his officials and encouraged initiative. They saw themselves more as associates rather than employees. They felt humiliated and insulted only by Tito's royal aspirations, by his autocratic prerogatives.

I have never been able to account for Tito's propensity for self-mythologizing. The explanation that it derives from his lust for power and glory has never seemed to me adequate. To be sure, Tito could not help but portray his achievements as extraordinary. He even made up a thing or two, stressing his superiority and magnifying the danger to which he was constantly exposed. But it was not for glory. Tito's self-mythologizing was naïve, sometimes childishly fanciful. Very rarely did it enhance his prestige and power. Could it be that his subconscious tendency was to view himself and his mission as the will and the whim of a higher force? I do not know. Tito's myth-making, in any event, never gave way to total fabrication: his fancy was always connected to something concrete, to some object, person, real event. It was always chance that controlled his political activity.

In 1946 Tito was operated on for a hernia by a team of Russian doctors. A year or so later, after the 1948 break with the Soviet Union, he told us that the Russian surgeon had been drunk during the operation. Some time ago, he said that a ring he wore during the operation had saved his life. How could a ring have saved his life? He was not referring to a ring he had once bought in the Soviet Union for possible conversion to cash in an emergency. That ring had slipped off his finger and was lost during the Fifth Offensive. No, the ring he was referring to was the ring the Soviets had given him when he visited Moscow in March of 1945. But since that time he had been in no mortal danger, and certainly not in the kind of danger from which a magic ring could have rescued him.

What did it mean, then? We were also told that during the Fifth Offensive a dog specially trained to nose out explosives had saved him from a German bomb! Several years ago, in reminiscing about our withdrawal after the German attack on Drvar on May 25, 1944, Tito claimed that a Chetnik by the name of Rodić had him, Tito, in the sights of his gun. How did Tito know that? He had probably heard that this Rodić had been prowling around in those parts at the time. But how would Rodić have known he was tracking Tito? It was inexplicable! Chance and risk—terrible risk. And so it goes. Except for his most slavish toadies, everyone took Tito's self-mythologizing as a harmless fantasy, a spiritualist game. Tito did not so regard it. He repeated certain myths about himself time and again, until they became strongly entrenched in his image of himself.

Tito needed to be the first to announce important news, he needed to be conspicuous, to be the master of mystery. While he was on a state visit to Poland in the spring of 1946, Ranković notified him by telegram that Draža Mihailović had been captured, and mentioned that the news could not be announced just yet, because Mihailović's accomplices were still in hiding and were being tracked down. I was in Poland with Tito at that time. Ranković's cable gave Tito special pleasure. A death blow had been struck to the Chetnik movement, and an end had been put to the heroic legend of Mihailović, which Western propaganda had blown out of proportion since the outbreak of the war. But Tito could not restrain himself, and with undisguised pleasure announced Mihailović's capture at a news conference.

Just two days prior to the Central Committee meeting of April 12, 1948, at which a reply was to be drawn up to the Soviet attacks on the Yugoslav Party, I was on my way home from the office and happened to ride past the Soviet Embassy near Slavija Square. Žujović's car was parked in front of the Embassy. Standing nearby was his mustached bodyguard. To double-check, I ordered my chauffeur to turn around and drive past the Embassy once again. Žujović was already under suspicion because of his pro-Soviet leanings, but he was not yet under surveillance. That same day, Kardelj, Ranković, and I met with Tito to discuss the forthcoming Central Committee meeting. I told them about Žujović's car. We were finally forced to admit that Žujović was acting in collusion with the Soviet Ambassador, Arkady Lavrentiev. At the Central Committee meeting, during a stormy debate set off by Žujović's acceptance of the Soviet criticism, Tito simply had to let the cat out of the bag: "Crni [Žujović's nickname], what were you doing at the Soviet Embassy the other day?" Žujović could not hide his surprise, but quickly regained control: "Well, we were talking about getting a car for Lavrentiev." At that point I remarked: "So a Yugoslav government minister performs services for the Soviet Ambassador." This haste to divulge privileged information seemed to be a component of Tito's self-mythologizing. Probably it also served a political purpose. It proved that Tito was omniscient and therefore omnipotent.

Was Tito's religious feeling linked to this? Did he have any such feeling? Since he was a Communist, naturally he was an atheist. But he was not just any Communist. His atheism was never militant. Indeed, it was never expressed as a deep conviction. Atheism was for him a component of ideology. In maintaining relations with the church, Tito simply made sure that the state remained dominant and was in no way undermined or threatened by the church. He did not believe in a fixed God or in the teaching of any religion.

Is there any point in discussing Tito's religious feeling? Absolutely. Religion encompasses guilt, an emotion that fluctuates, an emotion that bears on political imperatives and judgments. Religion also gives rise to doubt and reflection on human tragedy. Tito would not sign death warrants. The Yugoslav Constitution had always provided that this was the duty of the chief of state. However, at Tito's express orders, this responsibiltiy was shifted to other institutions. The actress Elizabeth Taylor was enchanted with Tito, mostly because she had heard that he had not signed a single death warrant. Literally, that may be true. For Tito, his signature on a death warrant would have had mystical powers, the powers of justification. Perhaps he felt that if he did not sign a death warrant, death would not be inevitable. In any case, he could not be held responsible for it, if it did occur.

It is superfluous to cite Tito's orders regarding capital punishment. There were many killings. It could hardly have been otherwise, given the power whose agent and captive he was, power that had become the cause of so much killing, so much death. For Tito, such killings were politics, that which must be done in the service of a fixed and premeditated goal. As long as circumstances permitted, he wanted to evade responsibility for someone's death. I prestige, but above all, the awareness of a change in polit- mad struggle with him. Tito may not have been the only one to save me. Ranković protected me, probably because of our long-standing friendship. I have been reliably in- formed that the apparatus, the secret police, recommended that the Djilas case be "physically resolved." But Ranković did not respond to that recommendation. Perhaps he did not even consider it. Other conditions worked in my favor as well: publicity in the West, the top men fearing to lose prestige, but above all, the awareness of a change in polit- ical tolerance following the confrontation with the Soviet Union, and particularly the new understanding of Stalin's bloody purges. C. L. Sulzberger told me that Tito denied his request to visit me in prison by remarking, "In the Soviet Union, they execute people for that!"—meaning what I had done.

Political expedience "eternally" suppressed Tito's reli- gious feeling. The feeling was unexpressed, disturbing, and it reasserted itself in the real and the transitory. In April 1953, on Tito's Blue Train, carrying Kidrič's body on its last journey to Ljubljana, the conversation turned to death and the inexorable passage of time. Kidrič's death, the first to occur among our leaders in peacetime, was inscrutable and shocking, and it led to the need for metaphysical assurances —flight from an emotional conundrum. I was saying that there was nothing beyond matter itself, indestructible and changing. Tito interrupted me: "Don't dwell on that now." Then he added, reproachfully, but with a smile: "Who knows what it is all about anyway, who knows?"

Although Tito's hallmark was power and struggle, he also

possessed an inborn, unconventional, nonideological awareness. Of the Austro-Hungarian Empire, he remarked more than once: "A good, organized state." When I commented on the despotic and melodramatic character of the later reign of the Montenegrin King Nikola, Tito objected: "Oh, no, we young people thought him charming, brave, patriotic, a true Yugoslav." Tito believed that the nationalities of Yugoslavia would ultimately merge into one true nation. When I remarked that King Alexander Karadjordjević thought so, too, he retorted: "Ah, but there was no socialism then." On that very same train that was carrying Kidrič's body, we talked about the forces that shape history. I attempted to explain history in terms of the most rudimentary Marxist teaching, which is to say, the ideas and the masses are the basic and decisive elements. Tito snapped: "Nonsense! Often the entire course of history depends on one person." It seemed obvious that Tito had himself in mind. The political leader must interpret doctrine in his own way, in his own image.

11

Tito tried to separate his private life from his political activity, yet he could not achieve more than partial success, for absolute power subjugates private life as well as everything else. His efforts to protect his private life were rooted in his European heritage of individualism, a heritage that no Leninist forms or ideology could extinguish. It also had its source in the human aspiration to intimacy, to personal happiness.

Well, then, was Tito happy? The wrong question! What is happiness? Especially, what is it to a politician for whom power is the highest good, if not the only good? Look at the question more broadly: Has there ever been a creator who is not under the illusion that he has created a world unto himself, yet who has not left that world a wasteland, who has not, in the end, destroyed everything that he ought to have loved?

It is not by chance that Stalin destroyed his family, sacrificed everything that was his. Tito learned chiefly from the confrontation with Stalin that absolute rulers last only as long as their power. Nadezhda Mandelstam observed of

Stalin that a tyrant is immortal while he is alive. Tito consoled himself that his absolute power would be justified if he could lead Yugoslavia, a backward and disunited country beset with dangers from abroad, with a dogmatic Party and a nondemocratic state machinery, to prosperity and independence. After the confrontation with the Soviet Union, Tito legalized his personal power, and so was able to moderate it. That was in accord with his charismatic mission. He had sprung from the roots of national suffering and rebellion. He strove for the original. He was attracted to royal splendor. His power was closer to Western absolutism than to Eastern despotism.

I have already established that Tito did not destroy, though he checked, the flow of ideological and social currents within the nations of Yugoslavia. He did not destroy his family either. On the contrary, his brothers and their descendants flourished. But he did not get close to his own family, to enjoy tranquillity with its members.

Tito had four wives. He was married to the first and the last, and had common-law marriages with the second and the third. These four women played important and different roles in his life, but not one—and I am sure even about the first one, though I know little about her—exerted any substantial influence on his life, let alone on his decisions.

He met his first wife in Siberia in 1917 or 1918. People maintain that Pelagia Belousova was then sixteen years old, twelve years younger than Broz. She is said to have been uncommonly beautiful. It is no accident that all Tito's wives were beautiful women, and all of them progressively younger than he.

In September 1920, when Josip Broz returned from the Soviet Union, he was accompanied by his young and beautiful Russian wife. She was also a Communist, although her political activities were never publicized in Yugoslavia. Broz and Pelagia had three children, of whom only one, the son, Žarko, survived. Nothing is known about the relationship between husband and wife. That is not accidental, because for Tito any reference to that marriage was painful. It seemed as if he wanted to blot out every trace of it from his life and his memory. It is implied in Tito's biographies that from time to time he lived apart from his family, but the reason for that may well be the circumstances imposed on him by the Party's illegal status, as well as his lack of any permanent employment.

Whatever the reason, a separation between Broz and Pelagia took place after Tito's arrest in 1928. She went back to the Soviet Union with their son—not unusual for a wife whose husband was arrested. In Russia, while her husband was still in jail, she remarried, and placed their son in a children's home. Partly because of his unruly temperament and partly because of Soviet pedagogical methods, the son took a violent dislike to school and became something of a vagrant.

After his release from prison, in January 1933, Broz went to Moscow. Party duties prevented him from spending as much time as he should have with the neglected boy. In the middle of 1936, he had to leave Moscow for Party work in Paris and Yugoslavia.

Did Josip Broz ever see Pelagia in Moscow? If he did, they renewed none of their previous ties. The purges did not spare her. And it was not until after Stalin's death in 1953 that she was released from camp. Tito had known Pelagia intimately. He knew what kind of an "enemy" she was, but he was evidently reconciled to her presumed guilt and suffering, all the more strongly and inexorably because of her unfaithfulness while he was sitting in jail for the revolution. That was a great blow to his male vanity. He felt her neglect of their son alone justified his bitterness and sorrow.

Tito never spoke of Pelagia. On several occasions, Kardelj warned me to avoid the subject. During the war, when Tito learned that his son had lost an arm in the defense of Moscow, he responded with tenderness and grieving pride. I happened to meet a Soviet emigrant from Moscow who had known Tito's first wife when she was released. He told me that Tito did not see her on his later visits to the Soviet Union. All she ever wanted of Tito was to be allowed to see her son and her grandchildren.

Tito's second wife was Herta Hass, a student from Maribor, in Slovenia. They met during the course of Tito's illegal Party activities in the spring of 1937. Herta was a soft, shapely brunette who radiated an inner warmth. She was deeply attached to Tito. The Slovenian Party officials who knew her well considered her bourgeois, probably because she stood out from the ordinary. She dressed neatly and spoke well. But she was a conscientious and devoted Party member. After the war, she married another man, had two daughters, and she now lives in Belgrade. Five or six years ago, I ran into her. (My wife saw her more often.) We greeted each other cordially. Despite veiled resentment when she spoke of Tito, she never let you forget that he was the father of her son and never said a bad word about him. She was always in control. I have heard that she refused to accept a medal from Tito, on the occasion of her sixtieth birthday or some other anniversary—an unusual and proud gesture.

Tito's break with Herta occurred in the spring of 1941. She was then recovering from the birth of their son Aleksandar (Miša) and taking care of him. Meanwhile, a young woman student was sent from Belgrade to Zagreb to attend an illegal course in radiotelegraphy. Her name was Davorjanka Paunović, but during the war we knew her as Zdenka. Tito probably suggested that typically Croatian name as a code name. Davorjanka had a boyfriend in Belgrade who was also a student and a Communist. He distinguished himself in the war and later became a prominent political official. The course in radiotelegraphy was given in an apartment in Zagreb, and Tito dropped in from time to time. That is how he and Zdenka got to know each other. By the time Tito and the Politburo returned to Belgrade, following the occupation of Yugoslavia, Zdenka and Tito had become inseparable. In fact, they stayed together all through the war. Zdenka served as Tito's secretary, although she was not particularly well organized or diligent. Neither was she brave, being far too nervous and apt to panic.

Zdenka was strikingly beautiful. Her feverish expression only served to accentuate her beauty. She was slender and well proportioned, with an olive complexion and large gleaming dark eyes. She had the exotic beauty of some Romanian women, and, given the Romanian minority in her native region, perhaps there had been some crossbreeding in her family with that ancient, pre-Slavic people.

When Tito appeared with Zdenka in Belgrade in the spring of 1941, he faced a puritanical Party, particularly the Belgrade division. One could change partners, but only after a previous relationship had been terminated. Otherwise, fidelity was expected, and one simply did not enter casually into another intimate relationship. That puritanism was a backlash from the free love of earlier generations. The encouragement and enforcement of puritanical standards and behavior did serve to strengthen the bonds of Party brotherhood and unity. Yet it led ultimately to tragic and absurd situations: one comrade killed himself; others were punished by the Party; still others had liaisons with bourgeois girls—but presumably the idea of such liaisons never crossed the minds of our female comrades.

Tito was aware of all that. He did not oppose it, though he was not, in contrast to Ranković and myself, an advocate of puritanism. Nothing was said about his relationship with Zdenka. It was not for another year, in fact until 1942, that I became aware of the nature of their relationship. Something in that situation was wrong. Herta was his acknowledged wife, by whom he had recently had a son. No one denied Tito's right to take up with another woman, but he should not until the relationship with Herta had been resolved. Yet no one said anything in public. Nor did Tito, not until circumstances forced him to.

Herta was clearly aware of her importance as the wife of the Secretary General of the Party, and it showed in her devotion to Tito. For Zdenka, her connection with Tito precipitated a struggle for prestige. She was constantly afraid she would be pushed aside. Her struggle was carried on relentlessly in wartime—in a guerrilla war, in forests and caves, in peasant houses and huts, when they were without food, when they were faced with death! But hell ignites rather than extinguishes passions and ambitions. Zdenka picked fights and made scenes, sparing no one, including Tito, at the most unexpected times and in the most unlikely situations—because someone dropped something, because someone brushed against her when passing, because she was not the first to be asked whether Tito was asleep, because the meat was overdone or underdone, because the smoke was blowing in her direction. No one liked her. No one even had a chance to like her, because she insulted everyone. It occurred to us that she might have become intolerable to Tito, but that he felt he could not extricate himself from that relationship because his position in the Party would suffer and because the puritans would reproach him for changing women. We even hoped he would return to Herta, although that would not have been in line with our puritanism, since he had not too long before thrown his lot in with Zdenka.

But we were wrong. With a great deal of trouble—and with the cooperation of the Germans, who included her in an exchange of prisoners—Herta was released from an Ustashi camp. She had been tortured and abused and had lived in constant fear of death. I brought her from Sarajevo to our headquarters in a forest in the spring of 1943. On the way, I said nothing to her about Zdenka, and it seemed that she knew nothing. She was overjoyed and happy to be free. But her joy and hopes collapsed the day we arrived. In a private conversation, Tito told her that Zdenka was his comrade now. He was in love with Zdenka and he acted in accord with Party regulations. Herta sobbed on my shoulder: "What is this, Comrade Djido?" But she accepted the break with the same dignity and patience as she endured one of the most difficult periods of the war—the Fifth Offensive. In the summer of 1943, she left Bosnia for Slovenia, again with me.

At the end of the war, Zdenka was struck down by tuberculosis. This smoldering illness must have accounted at least in part for her fits of fury, her frenzy, her idiosyncrasies. She was sent to the Soviet Union for treatment. After she returned to Tito at the White Palace, she was rarely seen. Her smile was sickly, as if asking for forgiveness. Zdenka died in 1946. At her express wish, she was buried in the garden of the White Palace, to remain close to Tito.

Tito was visibly depressed. When I asked Ranković what was wrong with the Old Man (the nickname Lola Ribar and I gave Tito in 1937), Ranković told me that it was because Zdenka had died. Not a single leading comrade attended her funeral, not because she was disliked, but because Tito had kept her death a secret. No one hears about Zdenka any more; it is as if she had not been Tito's closest companion and secretary during the war. Tito's biographers do not mention her. Wartime photographs of her have disappeared. A street in her native Požarevac bears her name, presumably on the initiative of local officials, certainly not Tito's.

Tito recovered quickly from that blow. Zinka Kunc Milanov, a star at the Metropolitan Opera in New York, had returned to Yugoslavia at the end of the war, and it was soon apparent that Tito took an interest in her. She made few appearances except at fund-raising concerts. She was an imposing, beautiful woman, famous at home and abroad. In his ascent to royal heights, Tito probably found Zinka's fame as seductive as her majestic appearance and the unsurpassed clarity of her voice. But she gave no sign of reciprocating Tito's interest, no response beyond politeness, beyond what any sophisticated woman would show a suitor of such stature. Moreover, she had just been married again, to a Yugoslav general by the name of Ljubomir Ilić, a fine revolutionary, his own man, celebrated for his activities in the Spanish Civil War and the French Resistance. A sudden new relationship would hardly have been appropriate, even had Zinka Kunc Milanov been tempted. And usurping the wife of one of his generals would hardly have enhanced

Tito's reputation, even had he been able to ignore the contempt and hostility of the Party matrons toward "foreign" women and particularly women of the theater.

Obviously, then, a new wife, a new love could be found only in Tito's immediate circle. His freedom of movement, officially and at leisure, was under the strict surveillance of his guards and his staff, who not only protected his life and helped him in his important work, but also saw in him the embodiment of Party heroism and morality. The new woman was Jovanka Budisavljević, who was in charge of his household. It was her task to attend to all the innumerable, unexpected details and small necessities that life imposes even in circumstances far simpler and more modest than Tito's.

Jovanka was around Tito all the time. She had no regular hours. By virtue of her position and duty, she was part of Tito's security guard and entourage. By 1946 some degree of intimacy had probably been established between Tito and Jovanka. Before she met him, Jovanka had not had a lover. She was twenty-three years old, born in 1923; Tito was fifty-five.

Jovanka was soon noticed, not only because of her appearance and bearing, but also because she was in attendance wherever Tito traveled or stayed. I was more observant this time than I had been with Zdenka. I decided that there was something between Tito and Jovanka. But I pretended not to be sure. In an effort to convince me, Koča Popović once said: "Well, why not? It's quite natural."

Jovanka was a striking beauty, a healthy Serbian beauty, with black hair, fair complexion. She was without coquetry, yet feminine. Her femininity was subdued. She was like a nun, or a peasant woman who has vowed to give her life to husband and children. Always dressed in the uniform of an army officer, because she was always on duty, she looked tall though in fact she was of medium height. At that time she was slender, and looked even more so in her tight-belted uniform. Under her slightly tilted Partisan cap was the silkiest and most luxuriant hair I have ever seen. She had large dark eyes, set off by the delicate flush of her cheeks, eyes full of patience, care, and devotion.

Jovanka had been selected for Tito's staff from the Sixth Lika Division. She came from a respectable Serbian peasant family. She had completed elementary school, which was, for children of that time—especially girls brought up in the remote and very poor region of Lika—decidedly a sign of above-average ability. In addition, at one time she had helped out in an inn managed by one of her relatives, which further qualified her for Tito's staff. Her major qualification, nonetheless, was her impeccable conduct as a soldier and her absolute loyalty to the Party.

It was a firm rule that only those who had been thoroughly checked out could serve Tito—any high official, for that matter. Titillating rumor had it that it was no accident that Jovanka had been selected by the security service for Tito's staff. They chose and delivered a politically impeccable girl, above all a beautiful girl, put her beside him and let nature take its course. Now and then, even I teased Ranković—of course, after Tito had married Jovanka, so that the jokes could hardly be construed as subversive—that his security agents had set it all up. Ranković denied it with a glint in his eye.

The relationship was unhappy and destructive, particularly for Jovanka. She had no life outside Tito's circle and the routine of her duties. Many evenings when we were visiting Tito, we would see her sitting in a hallway, keeping watch for hours with Tito's escorts, until Tito went to bed. Under such circumstances, envy and distrust from the rest of the staff were inevitable. Her intimacy with Tito could have been interpreted in any number of ways, not one of which was fair to her—careerism, sycophancy, female duplicity, lust, abuse of Tito's loneliness, greed. Occasionally the security men, out of malice or distrust, would force her to take the first mouthful of the very food she had lovingly prepared for Tito.

This state of affairs lasted for years—six long years of suspicion, malice, envy. But out of love and duty the young woman endured patiently. For her, Tito was a Party and wartime deity, and sacrifice was his due. But she was getting to know Tito as a man and found herself falling deeply in love. All during that time, she behaved with silent, unobtrusive patience—never a superfluous word, no fuss. She was determined to be consumed if need be, to wither, unknown and unrecognized, at the side of the deity about whom she had dreamed. She belonged to Tito only because he had chosen her.

Why did Tito insist on such a demeaning relationship? Because Jovanka, an uneducated peasant, was not sufficiently imposing? Because after three unsuccessful marriages he no longer hoped to find happiness in marriage? Did he want to remain free of any woman? Obviously, Jovanka bowed to his wishes and intentions. Was the tragedy of Jovanka's fate—Tito's final break with her, that inexplicable separation from her in his eighty-fifth year—rooted in such bitter beginnings?

A curious turn of events led to their marriage. In 1951, at the end of March or the beginning of April, Tito suffered an acute gall bladder attack. Doctors as well as the highest officials scrambled to his villa on Užička Street. Tito had suffered previous gall bladder attacks—he had to watch what he ate, and especially avoid his favorite smoked meats. This time the doctors discovered that the pancreas was affected. It might be fatal. The surgeon Lavrić was flown in from Ljubljana, and an operating table was set up in the dining room of Tito's villa. To test the condition of his liver, blood samples were taken every hour.

Ranković and I slipped into Tito's bedroom. Kardelj was there, too. Tito was lying in his bed, contorted with pain—brief cries alternated with gasps. We asked him one of those inane and useless questions that one falls back on in such moments. He retorted, in cruel pain: "Don't ask me anything! This is horrible! Just leave me alone!" Jovanka met me on the stairs. In the rush of events no one had thought of her. Controlling her tears, she asked: "What will happen, Comrade Djido?"

That was the first time Jovanka had addressed a member of the Politburo. While I was at the top, at any rate, she was respectful and modest toward the comrades of the leadership. We had already talked to the doctors, and I was able to reassure her. Later that same day, after conferring with Doctor Lavrić, whose confidence had relieved us entirely, I explained to Jovanka that the illness was under control. Should his condition get worse, he would be operated on immediately. Eventually, when he was in better shape, he would be operated on anyway; he could not risk another such attack. That was what happened. Tito was operated on at Bled on April 19, 1951, in a hospital the Germans had built for their wounded, which Tito took over after the war.

Jovanka's care and nursing of Tito during this illness were extraordinary, meticulous in every way, and cemented the bond between them. This bond, already obvious to those around Tito, now became open and natural. On the evening before the operation, the members of the Politburo and the doctors lingered after dinner in the drawing room. Although concerned about the operation, Tito seemed to be enjoying that warm, nonpolitical atmosphere. Jovanka was there, too, for the first time, elevated from the false and unnatural role of an attendant. She was still subdued and shy. Conversation turned to the subject of great men and their private lives, and Doctor Lavrić remarked, probably with the relationship of Tito and Jovanka in mind, "The private life of great men has no bearing whatsoever on the evaluation of their historical role." I did not agree with Doctor Lavrić, but neither I nor anyone else contradicted him: his remark encouraged and comforted Tito and Jovanka. The next day, Tito was successfully operated on. After the operation, he was cared for by Jovanka and a nun, without whom Doctor Lavrić, a Communist himself, would not operate on the Communist leader.

At the beginning of the following year, 1952, Tito married Jovanka. On that occasion I said to Tito: "You did well to marry her." To which he responded: "Well, yes! And you know, she is a person in her own right!" In June of that same year, I married Štefica, and Tito asked: "Where is that comrade from?" I laughed and said: "From Zagorje. I wanted to choose a woman from your native region." Tito laughed, too, and said: "Like hell you did."

Jovanka made her first appearance in public during the state visit of British Prime Minister Anthony Eden. She was excited and scared, like young girls in Russian novels at their first ball. The wife of the French Ambassador, an enormously charming and candid lady, called out to me at the reception: "It's one big honeymoon around here." These details are important only because they demonstrate the shift in the private lives of those at the top after 1948, as well as the change in relations with Western representatives. I am not at all sure that Tito would have married Jovanka, or that I would have taken Štefica as my second wife, if it had not been for the departure from Leninist dogmas, which gave our private lives a new freedom.

Jovanka and Štefica grew close at that time, and often kept each other company. If it had not been for that friendship, I would have known very little about her. Jovanka was an unknown quantity to the public, which knew her only from newspapers and television, parades and official ceremonies, at which she appeared wrapped in fur coats and laden with jewelry. She performed in accord with protocol, always with a smile, invariably dressed in opulent clothes.

Jovanka soon appeared overpowering—too much laughter, too much adornment, too much smugness, excess, excess. But it was that Jovanka who lived up to Tito's concept of his own prestige, Tito's form of power. She surrendered herself to that. She was the loyal wife, and she was herself carried away by the glitter of power, convinced it was as it should be. This was the Jovanka that most people, women in particular, disliked, even hated, and gossiped about. It is said that some were sent to prison for a year or two for telling stories about her. People vented their envy and their discontent, all that they dared not vent on Tito, on Jovanka. With her loyalty and simple-mindedness, she made herself vulnerable.

Yet she was neither stupid nor evil. She had a methodical intelligence. After marrying Tito, she attended a special secondary school and graduated with honors, but not because teachers were intimidated by who she was. She worked hard. Only in public did she appear stiff and ill at ease. She worried about how she looked and what people thought about her. Her peasant background was neither an advantage nor a disadvantage. Class origins had ceased to be an issue.

During the time I was an official, Jovanka did not get involved in political disputes, let alone in decision-making. Her sector was her home and her husband, Josip. Order and comfort prevailed. However, Tito was quite sharp and cynical with her, even in the presence of others. She bore it in silence and with humility.

Tito's sons did not like her, though she held nothing against them. But they were not on good terms with Tito either: his elder son, Žarko, was wild, and Miša was bitter. Jovanka tended to her two younger sisters and helped them get an education so they could become independent, but she did not seek favors for them, though she could have done so.

Jovanka wanted to have children, but Tito would not consent. Perhaps he thought that children were unrewarding, or maybe he simply did not want further obligations. Jovanka suffered.

Forced to live at heights she could not conquer, and for which she was not equipped, Jovanka rapidly succumbed to the dazzle of power and fame. She befriended artists, journalists, and film makers. It is said she suggested Tito, and even herself, as proper subjects for films.

Yet I do not believe that she was engaged in political activity behind Tito's back. When their separation was announced, I tried to convince foreign journalists it was absurd to believe that she was engaged in political activity. They were nonetheless determined to believe widespread rumors that Jovanka was scheming with Serbian generals, that she was pro-Soviet, that she manipulated appointments and dismissals of the highest officials. She was alleged to have shown displeasure at the neglect of her impoverished region, Lika. It needs to be explained that Lika, inside Croatia, has suffered from the enmity between Croatians (Catholic) and Serbians (Orthodox). People said: "The Serbian blood in her has awakened."

What had awakened in Jovanka, I believe, was her wounded and battered pride. Most probably her awakening was triggered by a trivial matter, and she recognized that the sacrifice of her youth and her life was meaningless, that her own ideology had been betrayed, that her deity had feet of clay. In spite of herself, Jovanka had become an outcast, and suddenly everyone was sympathetic, except for Tito's camarilla, who were delighted at her demise. In his last years, the rumor went, Tito made every effort to avoid Belgrade, and Užička Street in particular, so that he would not run into Jovanka.

Where is she now? What is she doing? How does she live? Is there a deadly secret to come out of this feudal court? Tito's sons were at Tito's sickbed—the sons whom he so rarely saw, and who had never been involved in his work and his life. On his deathbed, Tito was more lonely than ever. Žarko and Miša. Žarko, who took after him in looks and temperament; Žarko, whose excesses so tortured Tito; Žarko, who finally found peace in family life. Miša, who withdrew into his work and his own circle. Žarko and Miša —Tito's own blood, after all is said and done. The rumor that Jovanka was at Tito's bedside during his final illness cannot be substantiated.

Tito lay dying, sustained by machines, surrounded by an impersonal staff, in the company of toadies and leaders of his own creation. The renowned wartime and Party leaders were gone, dead or banished or in disfavor—literally in disfavor, the feudal court once again. In his uncertainty and loneliness did he know, did he realize, that everything he had created was threatened? Perhaps he consoled himself: Something will remain. Even now, he might have said, they are celebrating my birthday with the marathon. Yes, that will remain, and that is my happiness.

12

"You are a different man," Tito said to me at our last meeting, in early January 1954 in the White Palace. Kardelj and Ranković were also present. I had requested the meeting with Tito by letter, partly at the suggestion of friends, partly out of political expediency. But I did not prove to be farsighted or adept at political manipulation. The meeting did not turn out the way I had expected. It was a prelude to the sentence that would, within a few days, be pronounced at the Third Plenum of the Central Committee: I would be ordered to submit my resignation as president of the National Assembly, an indirect but clear threat that I submit to "what must be."

"You are a different man." Those words are imprinted on my memory for all time, although even today, I still do not know what they meant. If I remember correctly, Tito uttered those words in the context of a remark by Ranković that I had not accepted the decision to change the name of the Party to the League of Communists. But I had accepted it! Or was it in the context of Kardelj's surly contention that I had ventured too far into reformism of the worst kind

—Eduard Bernstein's. What Tito implied, I suspect, is that when I get an idea into my head, I cannot give it up, that I do not know how to give in, or am unable to do so.

Tito's words concealed the source of my break with him and at the same time explained it: he and I were so radically different that only a shared ideology could keep us together. He and I often disagreed during our long association, but never about major political issues. Most often, the friction was an emotional clash on points of style. Until my fall from power, I had written more about Tito than any other writer except Vladimir Dedijer, who had written a full-length biography. I mentioned this to Tito at our last meeting, again for sentimental reasons, with the desire to soften the blow. The fact remained, however, that I could not change my views. I wrote about Tito in the spirit of the personality cult of the time, but also out of conviction. After the confrontation with Stalin, I attributed to Tito democratic impulses and initiatives. Actually, I hoped for these more than I honestly believed they existed.

In my sparring with Tito, differences in style, approach, and performance played a greater role than differences in character. Like Tito, I was adamant in defending my creation. At our last meeting, I said to him: "I understand. You created something and now you defend it. I have just begun. But I don't understand those two." I meant Kardelj and Ranković. Tito softened, but only for a moment, then proceeded to settle accounts.

Minor quarrels between Tito and me had been of no consequence because they were not political. I loved and respected Tito. And I loved and respected him more as the years went by. I cannot recollect ever being disloyal to him. If I had a bad thought I would suppress it, reject it, get to work and carry out the task at hand. Tito was never hateful or treacherous to me—not until we were divided politically. There was nothing personal about our only, and last, political quarrel, unless, of course, you are unable to separate ideas from the people who hold them.

The roots of confrontation lie in our characters and to that extent in our styles. For Tito, idea and deed were inseparable from personal ambition and prestige. As I see it, I am idea and deed; consequently, I am indifferent to prestige. If anything, prestige bothers me. So long as I was convinced that Tito's activity consolidated idea and deed, his autocratic and intractable style was not at issue. Of course, I did not always approve of that style—I may have nagged—but in the end I did what I was told and even took initiative in developing Party policies.

Our parting began with our victory and our rise to power. A tiny seed of doubt was planted in my mind: this is not what we thought it would be, but maybe it is the beginning of our future. There was dissatisfaction, too, dissatisfaction with oneself, one's aspirations, and one's prospects, a dissatisfaction which, like fog, now thickened and now and then dispersed. Probably I would have gone back to writing and accepted life if the Stalinist storm had not turned everything upside down and revealed the monstrous face of oppression and conquest.

If someone had asked me six months before the eruption of our antagonism whether I could conceive of a force that could separate me from Tito, Kardelj, and Ranković, I would have said no. Not even death, I would have said, could do that.

The Yugoslav leaders, Tito foremost among them, anticipated that Stalin's death would generate a scramble for power in the Soviet leadership and that the threat of aggression against Yugoslavia would subside. This was exactly what happened. Tito immediately grasped the situation and seized the opportunity to block democratization, primarily in the realm of ideas. In so doing, he subjugated once and for all the Central Committee and the Party to his personal power, and undermined the role of the oligarchs, especially the ideological oligarchs, those torchbearers of heresy.

The moment of truth occurred at Brioni in the summer of 1953, at the Second Plenum of the Central Committee, at which time Tito put an end to the struggle "against bureaucracy," in other words, he put an end to the struggle for democratic reforms. Before that secret Plenum, Kardelj had told me that Tito had anticipated a change in our relations with the Soviet Union. The possibility of such a change made me uncomfortable, though I could not say exactly why.

It was not until the late fall of 1953 that I realized how quickly the discord among us was growing. I continued to publish proposals for reforms at a feverish pace. Objections began to trickle down from Tito and his group at Brioni. Kardelj was decidedly cautious and reserved.

From the end of 1949 to the summer of 1953, the Yugoslav Party leadership had been in the throes of spiritual liberation from the constraints of Soviet models and doctrines. Not only did the majority of Party theoreticians—Kardelj, Bakarić, Pijade, myself, and others—feel free to criticize the Soviet system, but also we had turned our attention to assessing Yugoslav reality. That was a period of intellectual boldness and spiritual freedom, which the Yugoslav Communist movement was not to experience again. The power structure, the control of the secret police, and the political monopoly of the Party had not changed fundamentally; but willfulness and lawlessness were limited, and doctrinal rigor was relaxed.

I myself overestimated the depth and scope of the democratic process. I believed that now that our leaders recognized the nonsocialist nature of the Soviet system, and of our own system in a milder, imitative form, they would act accordingly. I did not arrive at my point of view suddenly, or independently of the mood that prevailed at the top. Tito gauged that mood, too, but he moved with caution and circumspection, as always when it came to a theoretical turn of events. Ranković was the only major leader who was not intoxicated with democratization. He accepted it and put it into practice, not out of conviction but mainly because he was a disciplined Party member.

On one occasion—I believe it was in 1952—Tito cried out, as if he were just remembering something important: "We will not have a multiparty. We will have a multigroup system!" This is only significant as an illustration of the climate generated by our confrontation with the Soviet Union. In his criticism of the Soviet system, and in his evaluation of our own bureaucracy at the Sixth Congress in the fall of 1953, Tito went a step farther. Later, in the nineteen-seventies, during the period of bureaucratic reaction, he said that he did not approve of that Congress! In the spring of 1953, impressed by the discussions he had had with Swedish Socialists, who were guests at the Congress of the Socialist Federation, Tito said to me: "We should join the Socialist International as soon as possible." If this was Tito's thinking, one can only imagine what such Party liberals as Bakarić and Kardelj were thinking.

Tito was not in Belgrade in early January 1954, when the Politburo decided that the case of Comrade Milovan Djilas should be discussed at the Third Plenum, scheduled for January 18. No meeting of the Executive Committee was actually held. Kardelj and Ranković conducted their consultations chiefly over the telephone. The order itself came from Tito, of course. No one notified me about the Plenum. I read about it in the newspapers.

At that time, I was seeing a good deal of Kardelj and Ranković. It was with Ranković that I first felt an estrangement. For some time, I had been writing articles every Sunday for *Borba,* in which I debated issues I considered important for democratization, for Yugoslav socialism. Those articles were the reason for the convening of the Third Plenum, and for my subsequent conviction. One afternoon in late December of 1953, I went to see Ranković. We had been close through all of the critical phases of our lives—in the prewar underground, in wartime, and in anti-Soviet struggle. On this occasion, too, he was warm and friendly. He even offered me a hunting rifle as a gift. But in conversation, he was ominously reticent. Although I liked the rifle, I did not accept it. What is the sense in taking it, I thought, when we are obviously going our separate ways? When I asked Ranković directly what he thought about my articles in *Borba,* he answered me just as directly: "I hope I'll never have to bother with philosophical ruminations, but let me tell you that what you've written in *Borba* is detrimental to the Party." He did not surprise me. He had made it clear that he opposed reforms that could jeopardize the monolithic structure. In this he was straightforward, and he never took any treacherous action against me.

The meeting with Kardelj did surprise me. I was convinced that both of us were exponents of the democratic process. Indeed, so he was, until the Devil came to claim his due, until he caught a whiff of Tito's resistance and overnight transformed himself into a prosecutor who alerted Tito to danger and sought his intervention. Moreover, as a proponent of democratization, Kardelj had a decided advantage over me, if not in style and originality, then certainly by virtue of his reputation as a theoretician and because of his more responsible position. In late 1952 and especially in 1953, however, I believe I surpassed him in the range and the freshness of my ideas. Kardelj felt threatened in his role as the irrefutable Party theoretician, particularly because he knew that in a monopolistic hierarchy a weakening of his role would automatically mean the weakening of his authority. That, I am certain, cast the die with Kardelj. When I remarked that he and I were in agreement, Kardelj retorted: "No, we are not! I don't agree with you! You want to change the entire system!" I was alone. Alone, I made my decisions.

One afternoon, in early January, security agents tracked me down at the Kinoteka cinema. My wife, Štefica, thought that they were arresting me. That in itself was an indication of what the atmosphere was like. But I was sure that was not the case. The security agents told me to report to Kardelj immediately, and so I did. At Kardelj's, there was no discussion, no persuasion, no compromise. Ranković was there, reticent again, though now, I would say, showing not only resolution but also a touch of anger. I was not informed that the Plenum was to be convened. Conversation was ambiguous, murky. They remarked that the Old Man was angry, that my case was serious, that things could not go on as they were.

Kardelj said: "That's revisionism, in essence, the same as Bernstein." I replied: "I haven't read Bernstein, except for what I've picked up from Lenin." Kardelj said: "I've read him. Here, I've got a copy!" Finally, when I asked what he was working on, whether he was writing, he waved a half-written page in front of me and replied with a smile: "I am."

I gathered that he was writing something against me, a report for the Third Plenum. Yet I was told nothing about the Plenum or the report! Ranković left to attend to other business. I stood with Kardelj in the hall. Could he have suspected that his study was bugged? With an air of sincere, grave resignation, Kardelj said: "Nothing in my life has ever been more difficult." He made a gesture with his hands, as if to say, What can one do? He turned to go upstairs. Two or three months earlier, apropos of one of my comments, he had exclaimed passionately: "Maybe we shall gradually arrive at an opposition. . . ." And he had added: "As far as I am concerned, it would be best if this Party"—he meant the League of Communists—"did not exist."

That is Kardelj for you: resourceful, clever, tolerant, civilized, cunning. Cherishing a secret desire for what is democratic, even holding those democratic ideas, but without the guts to fight for them, to sacrifice for them. Why couldn't he sacrifice for them? Not because he cherished comfort! Maybe he sought power. It was Leninist pragmatism, the most effective pragmatism, free of bias. Kardelj practiced the theory of truth, that without organization and without power, ideas are little more than a pipe dream. He was poised between dictatorial power and dreams of freedom. Perhaps because he was a rational, practical Slovenian, Kardelj could not succumb to madness. Surely, he could not allow himself to be diverted by a mad Montenegrin.

Tito did not take his break with me lightly. I do not have to prove that. He was too shrewd not to know that he was walking the razor's edge of a profound shift toward unmitigated autocracy. That must have become particularly clear during the Plenum at which my deviation was aired, especially given the response in the Western press and public opinion at home. At our last meeting, he remarked: "This is the most important event since the confrontation with the Cominform in 1948. Look at the coverage the Western press has given it!" And when I dropped by the offices of the news agency Tanjug, I went away split right down the middle, pleased that my case was receiving so much attention and horrified to see the bourgeoisie and the reactionaries rushing to my aid. Clearly, I was still a Communist and an idealist.

The first news of Tito's displeasure and antagonism reached me through General Peko Dapčević, with whom I was on cordial terms. He had visited Tito on official business just before New Year's Eve, 1954, and Tito had commented unfavorably on my writing. Dapčević did not altogether grasp the implications of Tito's response. Tito was known to flare up. But I had no illusions. I knew I was in a vacuum. The more conservative comrades were avoiding me and making insinuating remarks.

The meeting with Kardelj and Ranković did not take me wholly by surprise. But the convocation of the Plenum, called without my knowledge, did disconcert me. I had hoped that should the dispute come out in the open, it would be discussed without acrimony and without the customary accusations that result from siding with the enemy camp. That was why I had suggested to Kardelj and Ranković that the matter be resolved within the Central Committee, without public hearings, and of course with the provision that I be permitted to defend my position. My proposal, and my suggestions, which were ignored, came to this: that I withdraw eventually from the Executive Committee, but stay on the Central Committee, with the option that I might continue to present my views in public—in a moderate but not officially approved form.

My proposal met with no response. Neither Tito nor the conservative, Leninist faction that held the reins of power with him was prepared to consider it. A monopoly of power inevitably imposes a monopoly of ideas. Nor could Tito or that group have reacted other than with unyielding and total condemnation. Their monopoly was threatened. They were single-minded and unilateral, and their methods fearsome and uncompromising.

Though Tito was sympathetic to the mood of that group, he did not quite share it. He had absolute power, but he refused to be branded as a dictator, particularly, a dictator in the Stalinist mold. Better than anyone, he knew that I was not an enemy or a traitor. What is more, he knew that I did not organize factions. At our last meeting, he conceded: "There's nothing organized in it." Indeed, even if I could have, I had no desire to form any group or faction. I sought to promote the free exchange of ideas, which, if extended to the League of Communists, would influence decisions and the movement toward a democratic society.

Beyond the political damage exacted by our clash, I believe that Tito found it hard to take psychologically, all the more so when the political penalties became obvious. At our last meeting, when I asked him to order some coffee for me because I had not been sleeping, he did so with an aside: "Others are not sleeping well either!" He looked tense and exhausted, as did Kardelj and Ranković. The quartet—Tito, Kardelj, Ranković, and I—which had guided the Party through great storms and set it on its independent course was disintegrating. So was Party unity and trust.

Even after the Plenum, at which I was indicted and condemned, Tito still had problems. With foreign newspapermen he would recall our mutual love and express regret that it had to come to this, but he stressed that I was politically dead: "That is the most terrifying death of all." When I read that, I was possessed by something atavistic, something rooted in my Montenegrin blood: "Not quite. Not as long as I am alive."

Once he had made up his mind, Tito did not waver. On the eve of the Third Plenum, he solicited one by one those Central Committee members who were known to be hesitant, or whose views were close to mine, and by invoking Party unity, the interests of the country, by implying subtly but unmistakably that he had the support of the army and the secret police, he managed to win them over, almost to a man. On January 17, 1954, following my distracted self-criticism, and an expression of guarded support from my former wife, Mitra Mitrović, and Vladimir Dedijer, the Third Plenum rendered its verdict. I was not yet formally expelled from the Party. Tito knew that expulsion at this time would provoke adverse reaction in the foreign press, and would be interpreted as resembling the Soviet way of doing things. Two months later I resigned from the Party.

In February 1954, soon after the Third Plenum, Dedijer came to see me at my villa in Dedinje. (I had still not been evicted.) It was sometime after eight o'clock in the evening. We took a walk in the garden, though it was very cold. We talked for about two hours. He was rather vague, but he told me that he had spoken with Ranković seven times. He did not refer to the substance of their conversations. From Tito's letter to Aneurin Bevan, published in Michael Foot's biography of Bevan, it is obvious that at the time Tito considered only me—and not Dedijer—a dissident. Three or four times that evening, Dedijer said to me emphatically: "They"—he meant the Party leadership—"would agree to talk with you if you would ask for a meeting." But he understood my response. After what I had gone through at the Plenum, and given the campaign that had been launched against me by the Party, I was not about to request such a meeting.

I had asserted myself politically and emotionally. The break with the leadership, with so many close friends, above all with Tito, Kardelj, and Ranković, was incomparably more devastating for me than any clash over ideas. But the humiliation I had suffered at the Plenum, the shabbiness with which I was treated, the slander and libel, took their toll. I felt totally alienated. At the Plenum, Tito reproached me for not having absorbed criticism, like Comrade Kidrič. The memory of Kidrič, his last horrible illness, his impressive funeral, was still fresh in my mind. Why should I have absorbed criticism like Kidrič?

I knew that *they* knew what was going on. In my mind and in my heart, I knew that what was happening to me was what happened to all Communist rebels within Communism: all were falsely accused, all recanted, all consented to their own self-destruction just so they could remain Communists.

It was not until well after the Third Plenum, perhaps a week later, that I was able to collect my thoughts. Sleep helped. I finally understood that not only was I rushing from defeat to defeat—that was not so important, since I had already been defeated—but also I would rush headlong into moral decline, into collapse, if I did not sever myself from Communism as an ideology. Tito, Kardelj, and Ranković would always press me to demonstrate my loyalty to the Party and to Communism. For Communists it is the only way! At the Plenum, after my self-criticism, Tito had remarked: "We'll see how authentic this is."

That is why I could not have responded in any other way to Dedijer's suggestion. For the same reason, when Dedijer proposed a year later that I organize my ideas and present them in a systematic form to the leadership, I had no choice but to decline: "That would only be to criticize Communism," I said. At this he fell silent and looked at me in dismay.

After the Plenum, I was in the throes of a moral and intellectual crisis, the heir to the legacy of suffering of my family and my native Montenegro, now embarking on a profound and as yet undefined experience. I realized that until that time I had fought with hesitation and under illusions, illusions about the leading Communists, about the integrity of their intellectual and moral values, about their friendship and their loyalty. My chief opponent, though not my only one, was Tito. I could no longer rely on his mercy or his understanding. Camaraderie and Communism, sincerity and loyalty, equality and freedom were dead.

Now that Stalin was gone, I suspected that Tito would normalize relations with the Soviet Union. In truth, I saw it happening in the fall of 1953. The Soviet chargé d'affaires noted that articles such as my "The Beginning of the End" were hardly conducive to normalization. Those at the top did not exactly deny it. In a preelection speech that same autumn I indirectly challenged the assumptions of normalization, including renewed cooperation of the Yugoslav and the Soviet Parties. For me, the break with Stalin had meant a break with the Soviet system.

In my break with Tito and the other leaders, relations between Yugoslavia and the U.S.S.R. were a secondary issue. But had I remained in the leadership, I would not have

accepted cooperation between our two Parties. The normalization of relations between our two governments was
useful and inevitable, but cooperation between our two
Parties was detrimental and destructive for Yugoslavia.
The Soviet leadership received the news of the action
against me with malicious glee. Gestures of reconciliation
became more frequent on both sides. In undermining my
revisionism, the Yugoslav leadership also rejected my theory
of the Soviet system as state capitalism. In 1955, when
Khrushchev visited Belgrade, he suggested with his characteristic heavy-handedness that the Yugoslavs pave the way
for a rapprochement with the Soviets by eliminating the
enemy: "You [eliminate] Djilas, we [eliminate] Beria." The
Yugoslav Ambassador to Moscow, Veljko Mićunović, re-
counts in his memoirs, *Moscow Years,* that during the Hungarian uprising of 1956 the Soviet leaders congratulated
him on my arrest.

It must have crossed Tito's mind that the clash with me
would be received favorably in Moscow, but that was a
secondary, minor consideration. The settling of accounts
with me would have occurred regardless of relations with
Moscow. Even before the death of Stalin, Tito was outspoken against any loosening within the Party, any breach
in ideological unity. If reconciliation with the Soviet Union
was a secondary issue in my clash with the Party, there can
be no doubt that my subsequent imprisonment was due to
the determination to improve relations with the Soviet government. I was twice convicted, and imprisoned for a total
of nine years. Certainly, there were other motivations: to
intimidate the ambitious, dogmatic, and liberal Party leaders, and to halt the legalization of any opposition. But the
Soviet connection was influential. It was as if there were

some fatal, unfathomable tie that still bound Tito, who only a few years before had so boldly resisted the Soviet assault.

I have been tried five times—once in the Kingdom of Yugoslavia, and four times under Tito—if I do not include the Third Plenum, which was a unique ostracism. One of those convictions, the one in 1956, with a sentence of three years of imprisonment, was based on a statement and essay I wrote supporting the Hungarian uprising. Another, in 1962, with five years of imprisonment, was based on my book *Conversations with Stalin,* published on the eve of Andrei Gromyko's visit to Yugoslavia and during the phase of brotherly friendship with Khrushchev. Both imprisonments were undeniably inspired by a desire for good relations with the Soviets, particularly because the convictions dwelt on accusations of "enemy propaganda" and "revealing state secrets." The absurdities of life and politics! In order not to provoke a foreign government, a comrade is put on trial—a comrade who energetically fought for independence from that very foreign government! While I was in prison, that absurdity, that travesty of camaraderie, made me occasionally bitter, but it also awakened and nourished my self-awareness.

Did I have to rebel? Did I make a mistake? Did Tito make a mistake? Only history will tell. Not before the break, and certainly not since, did I ever harbor any illusion or hope that I might seize power. I do not say that occasionally I did not crave power. It was no accident that at my meeting with Kardelj in early January 1953, I said that I did not have real power. My words had a double edge: I meant that I did not make decisions, that I exerted no substantial influence within the power structure. Kardelj replied sarcastically: "Oh yes, you did, and how!"

No matter how often I analyze my motives, after all these years, I come to the same conclusion: I was obsessed by certain ideas and certain realities which, even had I wanted to, I could not have abandoned without internal collapse. Those ideas were linked with my urge to write, to create something of my own. Moreover, those ideas and that urge were inseparable, contingent upon each other. How is it possible to create without ideas? Can ideas survive if they are not renewed, articulated? I believe that from the very beginning Tito sensed in me an unyielding opponent; he also recognized that I was in the grip of something irresistible and far-reaching. He was a deeply intuitive man. There is no other way I can explain his duality, his fury and his anguish over my disloyalty. Eventually, as the monolithic power structure eased, and in response to support for me in the West, Tito modified his position, although he could not suppress his rage whenever my name was mentioned. And what of myself? Because of my obsession with ideas, I could not manage the tactics of secrecy or manipulate power, though I was tempted by both.

That was it. I lacked political sense. I lacked an instinct for subtle, gradual far-reaching political strategy. Because of this I have often been criticized both at home and abroad. It was my conviction, however, that someone should initiate criticism, ideas, and that it should be me, since no one more responsible, more gifted, had attempted to do so. My ideas were not really all that original, not even for Yugoslavia. I felt that I was giving voice to something that emanated from everywhere. Unprincipled and conniving tactics and strategy were contrary both to my ideological focus and to my impulsive character. Whenever I thought of such tactics, they seemed to me remote and impracticable. The circle in which I moved was a narrow one, composed of comrades who knew each other so intimately they could read one another in the implications of an involuntary gesture or some nuance in the voice. The bond was forged in bloody struggles and friendship, rather than through ideas. Moreover, Yugoslav Communists were more open, more friendly, and more rational than their Soviet counterparts. In such an atmosphere, to pretend is not only dishonest, it is also impossible.

I had no choice but to follow my conscience. The alternative was to lie low, to abandon my convictions, to rot in the stifling and sterile service of a leader in whom one no longer believed, a leader who identified and subjugated the ideal and the nation to his own power and glory. Some who were skillful in the manipulation of strategy, more in love with power than I, remain in the Central Committee. What have they accomplished?

I made my choice in accord with my vision, my ability, and my conscience. I am convinced that what I did was right, although I am unconvinced that I shall win in my lifetime. That is the heart of the matter. There lies the difference. Tito is the victor. And Tito is not concerned with the vanquished.

13

Assessing the past is easier than predicting the future. Is this really true? New facts require new assessments. Thus, I can hardly render a final judgment on Tito. I cannot be impartial. Too much of my life was intertwined with his. But the fascination for storytelling lies in its infinite possibilties, its accretions of knowledge, its presentations of hypotheses in still another form, in the blend of the irrevocable past with the mutable present.

Tito clearly understood that he was not leaving an heir. Indeed, he made certain that there was none. He valued himself and his work to such a degree that toward the end of his life he ordered a constitutional change to introduce collective leadership, which insured that no one who came after him would command such power as he held, no one could ever use it to blacken his memory. In making his role impossible to duplicate, Tito sought to project himself into history. At the same time, he recognized that political forms are not permanently fixed. He provided a form that would, for a certain period of time, secure immortality for himself and his achievement.

I was seated at Tito's right hand during the ceremonies marking the tenth anniversary of the AVNOJ on November 29, 1953. Just before the celebration, Kardelj had mentioned that we had made no provision for a tribute to Tito on that occasion. We discussed whether this was the right time to unveil the "Marshal's seal," which the sculptor Avgustinčić had designed under Tito's supervision. I had suggested that the seal be the legal symbol passed on from president to president. But when I mentioned it to Tito, he, already annoyed by my revisionist writing, snapped back: "Oh, sure, so that some bum may parade it." Of course the seal might fall into the hands of some "bum," but that bum would be the president of Yugoslavia. Tito made certain that he, and everything that had to do with him, could not be equaled or surpassed. He believed that only historical splendor would remain in the national memory.

Tito did not shed his top people because he was afraid they would usurp his position or detract from his splendor. Rather, he shed them in the process of consolidating his absolute power. Only Kardelj survived politically, yet in the late fifties and the early sixties, he also appeared to be in disfavor. He hung on until his death, agreeing with Tito, adjusting to Tito's concept of a collective leadership in which Kardelj's own role was no different from anyone else's.

From the beginning, Tito's absolute power was sustained by people who derived their prestige and authority from the revolution. Power is Tito's legacy. However, in a one-party system, power is neither lasting nor universally effective. I do not advocate unchanging forms; still less do I believe effectiveness is based solely on absolute power. But even if the times were less turbulent, and Yugoslavia were not located in the Balkans, it would be to her advantage to have visionary and strong leaders and stable institutions. Collective leadership is contrary to the power Tito created and executed. His collective leadership will consist of Titoist Communists who, like Tito, have a noncollective concept of power. This form of leadership is contradictory and derivative. It was first practiced in the Soviet Union after the death of Stalin, as a reaction to Stalin's reign of terror, until one of the oligarchs seized power. He was Khrushchev.

Yugoslavia does not have either the internal or the external stability of the Soviet Union. Nor does it have a strong homogeneous ruling class. Yugoslavia is not a major power, nor does it have the potential to become an independent or imperial world power. The stability of Tito's Yugoslavia derived from the stability and absoluteness of Tito's personality. There is no comparable figure in Yugoslavia today. The structure of power is based on equality, on the equal participation of the republics in that power. By his autocratic superiority and authority, Tito insured harmony. The slightest disagreement now could provoke a great disturbance, which of course would be to the advantage of the Soviet Union.

Tito's achievement will probably be threatened where it is most vulnerable: in its ideological monopolistic authority. Consequently, Yugoslavia's independence will also be threatened.

But forecasts lie outside the scope of this book. Let us examine the reality Tito left behind, which will be attributed to his name. The first major achievement of Yugoslav Communism and its leader, Tito, was the revolution. This was the source of all later achievements, including the most important one, which was international in scope, the break with Moscow in 1948; it signaled the beginning of the dis-integration of world Communism into national states and national parties.

Of course, there are those who opposed the revolution it-self as evil and regressive. There are the Serbian nationalists who opposed it because it divided and disparaged the Serbian idea; there were Croatian nationalists who opposed it be-cause it disabled and subordinated their statehood; there were democrats who opposed it because it destroyed civil liberties. But the revolution is a fact of life, as are the changes that followed in its wake: equal administrative and cultural rights for all nationalities, and new social and eco-nomic relationships. The revolution did not quite solve the nationality question. It cannot be solved once and for all, because each nationality has a different internal structure and a different aspiration. But the revolution did initiate the development of separate nationalist statehoods within a federal community. Nor did the revolution resolve the so-cial issue altogether. That is not entirely possible. Such equalization would sap the vitality of society and condemn it to stagnation. New social relations gave rise to a new ruling class.

Tito and the Yugoslav Communists ought to be given a good deal of credit for what they did *not* do. Even though they leaned toward the ideological and emotional merger of all Yugoslavs—Tito's favorite slogan was "Brotherhood and unity!"—they did not inhibit the affirmation of state or cultural identities on a national basis. Something similar happened in the economy and the society. Industrial revolu-tion, which had its beginnings in the northern regions un-der Austrian rule, was greatly enhanced under Tito. As dis-tinct from the Soviet Union, Yugoslavia did not annihilate all nonsocialist forms and foreign involvement, in spite of the most advanced Leninist teaching, for an internally weak Yugoslavia would be subject to external pressure.

Independence, the break with Moscow, is indisputably the ultimate achievement to be attributed to Tito's name. The roots of Yugoslav independence lie in the power of the revolution. That independence expressed itself most fully in the initiation and implementation of a distinct foreign policy, notably the coming together of the nonaligned nations.

No matter which of these legacies we examine, we will detect incompleteness and inconsistency. The national economy suffers not only as a result of the world economic crisis, but also from an internal structural crisis which is insoluble in the present social and political context. There is low productivity; there is nonfunctional ownership; there is an ideological bias, on which administrative cadres are selected; there is an excessive exportation of the work force, which is now slackening as Western countries reduce their demands; there is the highest rate of unemployment in Europe, over twelve percent; there is the dependence of manufacturers on imported raw materials and semifinished products; there is an exorbitant debt and an excessive trade deficit. The officials themselves draw attention to the inertia of the League of Communists, despite the League's membership of one million, despite its long years of intensive indoctrination from elementary school to university, from factory workers to scholars in the Academy of Science.

Yugoslav society is pluralistic, stratified. Only the Party at the top is monolithic. I have already discussed the Party's utopian, ideological approach to self-management as a universal remedy. As for nonalignment, it is sufficient to point to the ineffectuality and discord of the "Third World" in all major crises (the occupation of Afghanistan, the Soviet-

Cuban interventions, the wars between nonaligned countries, and so on). The pro-Soviet states are among the most
heavily engaged in a nonaligned movement. Despite its
designation by its leaders (mostly dictators) as the conscience of mankind, the members of the nonaligned movement prove weak when it comes to power and money, to say
nothing of conscience. The nonaligned nations are in tur-
moil. Yugoslavia must find her own place, make her own
friends, and seek the means to preserve her political independence, the identity and freedom of the Yugoslav people.

Could Tito have done anything more or anything else—
burdened as he was by a Leninist Party, a Leninist ideology,
an autocratic power in a backward country devastated by
war and civil strife? The question is rhetorical. Under the
circumstances no more could have been done.

Could Tito have found forms and released energies that
would have produced better results? That gives rise to the
ultimate questions: Did such forms exist? Did such forces
exist? In other words, did Tito and Tito's Party stifle such
forms and such forces? If so, did they have to suppress
them? Here the question is one of freedom under Tito—not
theoretical freedom, or freedom conforming to a certain
model, but real freedom, the freedom that springs from the
vital forces of every nation. In that context, Tito's accomplishments are meager and regressive, deadly for the spiritual and material prospects of Yugoslavia.

No one will deny that in Yugoslavia the average man is
protected from lawlessness in his private life so long as he is
not involved in politics. But who is not involved in politics,
if politics touches on everyone and everything? So long as he
accepts his meager salary, he can survive biologically and
spiritually. That situation prevails in most of Eastern Europe. With regard to freedom, Hungary and Poland are not

so different from Yugoslavia. Yugoslav affluence and Yugoslav liberties derive less from Tito's liberalism—Tito never represented the liberal wing in the Party—than they do from the country's historic position and her natural resources. In Yugoslavia, life is undoubtedly better and more tolerable in most respects than in the other countries of Eastern Europe. Yet the situation is not as good as it could be if there was more freedom of expression within the ruling Party. The chances for such freedom are slim. The monopolistic nature of power, ideology, and politics suppresses other forces. I will discuss here only the most significant forces.

The democratic opposition was headed by Milan Grol, the leader of the Democratic Party, which was predominantly Serbian. Except for the Communists, all prewar parties in Yugoslavia were national—Serbian, Croatian, Slovenian. They disintegrated during the war. But some branches, except for those of the national-front groups, which yielded their autonomy to the Communists and abandoned independent organization, recognized the revolutionary changes and were willing to organize as a loyal, legal opposition. Not only did the Communist leadership refuse to accept that option, but also they resorted to fearful persecutions and harassment to eliminate the chance of any legitimate opposition.

In that, I played a prominent role in the area of propaganda, and I did so on my own initiative, solely because of the dangers of counterrevolution, even though counterrevolution was already essentially demolished and even though the army, the police, propaganda—in fact, all authority—were firmly in the hands of the Communists. The few remaining counterrevolutionaries mobilizing around Grol's Democrats did not have a chance. But the Communists extended the concept of counterrevolution to encompass all those who opposed them in any way.

We Communists did not want any opposition, none whatsoever. We wanted absolute power so we could rule more effectively and build a classless society without interference. In the summer of 1945, when the draft of the Election Law was discussed, we deliberately included provisions that rendered it virtually impossible for the opposition to participate in elections. We knew only too well the fragmentary and disorganized condition of the opposition! We knew we could cancel civil rights on the grounds of "collaboration with the enemy." The Party leadership made a realistic evaluation of our chances in an election, taking into account our wartime achievement, our organization, the popularity of Communists in the regions that had arisen in revolt. We estimated that we could win at least sixty to seventy percent of the vote. Nonetheless, we decided that the Election Law should be worded in such a way as to prevent the opposition from running in the election and establishing itself legally.

Grol had been vice-president of the government. He submitted his resignation by letter to Tito on August 18, 1945. That letter, which Kardelj brought to my attention, asserted that we had been willful, deceitful, and doctrinaire. The letter impressed us, the top leaders, more by its balanced, cultivated, and dignified tone than by the strength of its argument. For our consciousness, our forces, and our forms had long since become unilateral; we were firmly rooted in the one-party system. The democratic alternative was more than dismissed; it was annihilated. Our link with the political forms of the past was broken; and a new social order was set into motion which at every turn had to start at the beginning.

The interparty opposition to the Cominform, which emerged after the confrontation with the Soviet Union in 1948, provided no prospects for a democratic, pluralistic solution. Naturally, the opposing side, the pro-Soviet side, precluded that possibility altogether.

It was different in the early fifties. At that time, the various camps favored restructuring the existing social order, to ensure both a more dynamic political development and ideological independence. Because the suppression of that course coincided with the Party's squaring of accounts with me, those reforms are most often attributed to me. But actually a number of variables were at work, national, philosophical, and ideological.

In the late sixties, Yugoslavia had another chance, the most promising if also the most uncertain, at democratization with the rise of national Communism in Croatia (Mika Tripalo, Savka Dabčević-Kučar) and the democratic movement in the Party's leadership in Serbia (Marko Nikezić, Latinka Perović).

National Communism in Croatia did not rest on a specific political philosophy, but it was dynamic and realistic in its demands for autonomous rights, both civil and economic. Yugoslavia's shift from the cultural and administrative federalism of the Soviet type to a federation of republics with a certain autonomy is the direct result of the activity and resourcefulness of the national Communists of Croatia, who were joined by other Croatian nationalist segments. In time, the movement expanded. Tito himself could not figure it out. Later he claimed that he was being cheated. The Croatian leadership played on his vanity. It swore fealty to him. It extolled him in the press as a Croat and organized receptions for him. It enjoyed his support. But when it became evident that the movement was reaching unmanageable proportions, and that it was being overtaken by non-Communist forces, Tito dismissed the Croatian Party leadership, in December 1970, and ordered the arrest of the most prominent and most militant of the Croatian nationalists.

Something similar happened in Serbia, but the opposition there did not have massive support or nationalistic fervor. The Serbian opposition was composed mainly of intellectuals from the upper layer of the Party, the journalists and artists and writers. They did not articulate, or, more precisely, they did not get the chance to articulate, a clear ideological program. Obviously, they favored democratic methods. Whether they knew it or not, they were following the national liberal tradition of Serbia. They did not have real power—the police and the army were controlled from the center—and they were not organized. In any case, Tito called an illegal meeting of the Executive Committee of the Serbian Party; and when he could not muster a majority there, he disposed of the Serbian opposition by eliciting the support of his men, who were drawn from the lower ranks of the Party and the secret police.

Similar purges in Slovenia and Macedonia eliminated the Democratic nationalistic segments there.

Could Tito have acted otherwise and not placed his achievement in jeopardy? That is the wrong question! Tito's achievement was self-contained, self-sustaining. Real achievement releases creative energies. In the early seventies, Tito more firmly than ever held back the movement for change. He forced creative social, national, and individual potentialities to revert to the simplistic, withered ideals of his youth: to party, to class, to Marxism, to indoctrination.

Tito was a politician of unique achievement within the framework of the Communist movement. But he was a major and irreparable failure within the broader scope of what is democratic and what is humane. He was a politician of formidable resourcefulness, unerring instinct, and inexhaustible energy, but he was so attuned to personal power that, in crucial moments, he suppressed the forces that would have enriched life, made it more open and more creative for the individual and for society.

Tito was a politician of staggering proportions and of great independence, but he created, I believe it will be seen, no lasting spiritual or institutional forms. Titoism will fade with time, if Titoism is understood to mean personal power, the enforcement of one kind of ownership, the monopoly of the Party bureaucracy, and the one-party system as the basis of internal unity and external independence. That process began with Tito's death. But Josip Broz Tito as a historical figure will transcend his death and accordingly be the subject of research and analysis for a long time to come.

Tito's achievement cannot be separated from Tito's personality. His personality is more arresting and more original than his achievement. And more enduring. Things would have been different if Tito had not measured and adjusted so many of the efforts of his Party and his nation to himself and, too often, to his weaknesses. When all is said and done, the achievement makes the man, not the man the achievement.

BIOGRAPHICAL NOTES

Vladimir Bakarić (1912–)
Leading Croatian Communist, one of the chief organizers of the Partisan resistance during World War II. He has since held high government and Party posts in Croatia. He is a member of the Presidium.

Eduard Bernstein (1850–1932)
German Social Democrat and political theorist who was one of the first Socialists to attempt a revision of Marx's tenets. He proposed a type of social democracy that combined private initiative with social reform.

Peko Dapčević (1913–)
Montenegrin Communist who was named chief of the Yugoslav General Staff in 1953. He was implicated in Djilas's opposition to the Party and subsequently demoted.

Vladimir Dedijer (1914–)
Editor in chief of the Communist Party newspaper *Borba* and a member of the Central Committee. He wrote two im-

portant accounts of Partisan history, *Diary* and *Tito,* both of which have been published in English. He broke with the Party in 1954 over the Djilas affair, and has since devoted himself to writing and teaching.

Stane Dolanc (1925–)
Leading Slovenian Communist who joined the Partisans in 1944. He has been a member of the Central Committee since 1965. In 1971–1972 he played a prominent role in purging the liberal elements in the Party in Croatia and Serbia.

Andrija Hebrang (1899–1948)
Prominent Croatian Communist and leader of the Partisan movement in Croatia during the war. In 1946 he was found guilty of wartime cowardice and collaboration with the Ustashi, and was relieved of all his posts. After being arrested while allegedly fleeing to Romania in 1948, he committed suicide; some sources claim he was murdered.

Edvard Kardelj (1910–1979)
Organizer of the uprising in Slovenia in 1941 and a member of the Partisan high command. He became a member of the Central Committee in 1945. A leading Party ideologist, he was for many years presumed to be Tito's successor.

Boris Kidrič (1912–1953)
Slovenian Communist who held high political posts during and after the war. He became a Politburo member in 1948, and was in charge of the Yugoslav economy from 1946 until his death.

Veljko Mićunović (1916–)
Montenegrin Communist, a member of the Central Committee since 1952 and of the Presidium since 1971. He was Yugoslav Ambassador to the Soviet Union from 1956 to 1958 and to the United States from 1962 to 1967.

Draža Mihailović (1893–1946)
Leader of the Chetnik resistance to the German occupation and opponent of the Partisans. He was captured by the Partisans in 1946, tried as a traitor, and executed.

Marko Nikezić (1921–)
Serbian Communist active with the Partisans during the war. He later served as Foreign Minister and Secretary of the Serbian Party. An advocate of liberal policies, he had to resign in 1972 and was expelled from the Party in 1974.

Ante Pavelić (1899–1959)
Croatian fascist leader, head of the puppet independent state of Croatia. At the end of the war he escaped and took refuge in Argentina and Spain. Allegedly, he died in Madrid in 1959.

Moša Pijade (1890–1957)
Prominent Party theoretician of Serbian Jewish origin. With Djilas he led the Partisan uprising in Montenegro in 1941. He was later a member of the Central Committee and the Politburo.

Koča Popović (1908–)
Serbian Communist who joined the Partisans in 1941. After the war he was chief of the General Staff, Foreign Minister, a Vice-President, and a member of the Presidium until 1972.

Alexander Leka-Ranković (1909–)
High-ranking Serbian Communist and member of the high command during the war. He was later Minister of the Interior and head of the secret police. A Politburo member since 1940, he fell from power in 1964, ostensibly for abusing his authority. He was expelled from the Party in 1966.

Ivan Ribar (1881–1968)
Prominent Croatian leftist before the war. He joined the Partisans in 1941, became a Communist, and helped organize both sessions of AVNOJ (Anti-fascist Council of National Liberation of Yugoslavia). He was President of the Presidium until 1955.

Ivo-Lola Ribar (1916–1943)
Son of Ivan Ribar, he was a member of the Central Committee, and head of Communist Youth during the war.

Mika Tripalo (1926–)
Croatian Communist, active in the Partisan war. He was a member of the Central Committee for Croatia for many years. An active nationalist, he was forced to resign in 1971.

Svetozar Vukmanović-Tempo (1912–)
Leading Montenegrin Communist and member of the Central Committee. He held high positions in the postwar government, most notably as Director of the Central Economic Commission.

Radovan Zogović (1907–)
Montenegrin Communist, journalist, and author. He did propaganda work for the Party during and after the war.

Sreten Žujović (1899–)
Serbian Communist and an early member of the Central
Committee and the Politburo. An organizer of the Partisan
uprising in Serbia in 1941, a member of the high command,
and Finance Minister in the postwar government, he lost
his office and Party membership when he sided with Stalin
in 1948.